Divinely Dysfunctional

McDougal & Associates

Divinely Dysfunctional

Unique on Purpose

by

Benton T. Thompson, III

Published by:

McDougal & Associates
18896 Greenwell Springs Road
Greenwell Springs, LA 70739
www.thepublishedword.com

ISBN 978-1-940461-63-2

Printed on demand in the U.S., the U.K. and Australia
For Worldwide Distribution

DEDICATION

It is in loving memory of my parents, Rev. and Mrs. Benton T. Thompson, Jr., that I write this book. I have lived and learned what a family is because of them. I salute, not only the heads of my family, but also all those everywhere who continue to strive, live and love, no matter what comes their way.

I had been an adult already for many years before I learned that my family wasn't your typical traditional family. My wonderful parents, Benton and Barbara (both now deceased), were married for forty years and together raised nine children. I had seven older siblings, three boys and four girls, and four years after my arrival, my parents had number nine, my baby brother Zachary.

I was just six weeks old when tragedy suddenly and unexpectedly struck our household and decreased our numbers. According to Tyrone, my next-to-the-oldest brother, it seemed to be a day like any other day. All the kids in the neighborhood were outside playing and having fun, when it started to rain. The rain began very lightly at first, but within a matter of minutes it had increased to a full-on flood flowing through the "holla." (That's West Virginian for the hollow or valley areas between hills). Such floods are still devastating in many parts of that state.

After quickly assessing the situation, Dad devised an evacuation plan. He and Tyrone would begin transporting us, one by one, to higher and safer ground at the local elementary school. That seemed to be doable as it wasn't too far. A chain link fence was all that separated our yard from the schoolyard.

The two of them began with the younger girls, Carol and Debbie, who were six and four respectively at the time. Dad held tight to Carol, and Tyrone held tight to Debbie, but it wasn't easy. While Dad was trying to cling to the fence and hold on to Carol, the rushing water and debris swept them both under, and Tyrone and Debbie suffered the same fate. He recalls bobbing in the water, gasping for air and thinking he was about to breathe his last. But suddenly he was snatched up out the water by our father, who had somehow grabbed hold of a utility pole that was half submerged. Holding to the pole with one hand, he had been able to reach out and pull Tyrone to him with the other.

It was several hours before they were rescued. Sadly, the girls, my two sisters, Debbie and Carol, didn't make it, and two weeks later we buried them. Carol's body was found that day, but Debbie's body was not found until a week later. And Mom would not have the funeral of one without the other.

Amazingly, the flood waters stopped short of entering our home, and the rest of us were safe. I have long wondered why the smallest and youngest member of the family at the time—myself—was spared that day. Tyrone has wondered the same thing. God obviously had a plan. At my mother's insistence, we immediately moved out of that house and to higher ground on the other side of town.

Through all of this, my parents were determined to keep the family strong. Over the years they had numerous opportunities to give up, yet they never did. This single event could have decimated their relationship and our childhood and how we viewed life in general. Instead, it defined us, both as a family and as individuals, for good. Dad later told us an allegory that illustrated his concepts on life. He said:

> "Imagine a situation in which all nine children were neck-deep in water, and each one was desperately trying their best to stay afloat. If one of us went under, we would all have the responsi-

bility to go and try to save that one who was in greater peril. Some say the first law of nature is self-preservation, but, as Christians, we must deny self in order to help or save another."

Dad and Mom, it is because of your strength that I continue striving today. I love you. Rest in peace!

CONTENTS

In loving memory of My Sister Dear

MRS. PHYLLIS J. THOMPSON WILLIS

September 7, 1952 - December 21, 2016

INTRODUCTION

A word that I hear used a lot in today's society is *dysfunctional*. This word is talked about on television, radio, Internet and even around the water cooler. It's used to describe a person or group of people, often a family, with issues. The dictionary defines *dysfunctional* as "not normal or not functioning properly." But in a world of 7 billion people and counting, where no two individuals even have the same fingerprints, how can what's "normal" be determined?

We are all unique. Consider also that no two people have the same dental imprint. Some are tall, some are small, some are thick, and some are thin. So what's normal? And what's abnormal? How is normal or abnormal determined? Who can determine whether a person is normal or not? What criteria is to be used?

I'm not suggesting that some behaviors aren't outside of acceptable lines. Some certainly are! I'm merely presenting the idea that everyone different from me or you should not automatically be labeled as "dysfunctional." Perhaps they are "diff-functional" (my word, which means that they function differently than others.) Left-handed persons were once considered dysfunctional ... until it was figured out that they function quite well with their left hand. And that is the only way they are different from right-handed people. Thank goodness left-handed people didn't stop functioning just because someone said they were "dysfunctional."

Your dysfunction doesn't determine your destiny, it prepares you for it! "Awkward," "unique," "unfamiliar," "non-traditional," "eccentric" and "different" are not the same as *bad* or *dys*. Bad behavior is when someone is harmed (or worse). The children of alcoholic parents are still children in every sense of the word, yet society has labeled them "dysfunctional." We need to start separating the condition from the person and stop making flat judgments about entire portions of society. No one should be labeled "dysfunctional" just because they grow up in a bad environment. There is still hope for them, just as there was for each of us.

Hope for those considered to be dysfunctional ... that's what this book is all about, hope for those who have been labeled by society and considered to be not useful, having no worth, being not much more than throwaways, unusable. The characters I write about here seemed to be dysfunctional but they were people just like you and me who found a hope that had been looking for them all along.

And hope is looking for you too. I pray this book helps bring the two of you together.

Benton T. Thompson, III

Your dysfunction doesn't determine your destiny, it prepares you for it!

CHAPTER 1

A MANIC PROGRESSIVE

Even identical twins have different identities.

*I*t was a beautiful fall morning, and the air was crisp and fresh. The large, aged trees were fully outfitted with exotic hues of red, yellow and orange. The sky was wispy and still. Leaves and acorns were being tossed about everywhere, as the squirrels and birds conducted their yearly fall treasure hunt. It was a balmy 64 degrees outside.

By many standards it was an absolutely perfect day. On the outside, that is! Meanwhile, in the sterile, cold, old hallowed concrete halls inside of the university, it was a different story. The atmosphere was very stiff, pensive and a bit unnerving, but that was about to change.

Down front, Professor Jones cleared his throat and began, "Umh! Hum! We are graced this morning and for the next eight sessions by a man who has proven his worth in the important field of healthcare. He has not only shown himself to be innovative and highly gifted in this area; he has also developed a team of men and women who are unusually sensitive to the needs of those they encounter and have a remarkable success rate in treating them. This has brought him (and them) a lot of attention, and deservedly so.

As you can imagine, a man of this caliber is extremely busy, so when he accepted my invitation to serve as guest lecturer for these classes, I was elated. Please join me in welcoming Dr. Christopher Divine.

Dr. Divine takes the podium and speaks:

Divinely Dysfunctional

Hello, I am Dr. Christopher Divine, but you can just call me Chris. I am grateful to your professor for the opportunity to present this series of lectures entitled "Good Dysfunction," and I hope you find them inspirational and even life-changing.

It seems that everywhere you turn these days, someone is talking about a person whom they say is "dysfunctional," someone who was disadvantaged by what did or did not happen during their childhood. Or they had a family member who was odd and had some sort of issues. In this case, the whole family is labeled "dysfunctional." But doesn't every family have someone like that, someone who isn't like everyone else. Perhaps they are a little odd or different, but does that make them somehow unfit for society?

Truth be told, everyone has a bit of dysfunction in their family. It may be an uncle, aunt, cousin, sibling or parent. Or, maybe it's you. Don't worry. Some of the greatest and brightest minds known to mankind had what was considered some "abnormal" behaviors.

Take, for instance, the well-known "Drum Major for Peace," Dr. Martin Luther King, Jr.

He was a big science-fiction fan who loved the TV series "Star Trek." Howard Hughes, one of the most well-known and wealthiest people in the world of his time, was obsessed with the size of peas, one of his favorite foods. He even had a special fork to sort them according to their size.

Did you know that Leonardo da Vinci, the famous artist who painted the Mona Lisa, was an illegitimate child? Yes, he was. Albert Einstein's mother was told that her son was "too absent-minded" and "would never amount to anything." And there are many more who had similar stories, some of them well-known and some not. But we all have a story, don't we?

Since we are all unique and no two individuals are exactly alike, how can it be determined who is dysfunctional? We each have a one-of-a-kind fingerprint, as well as a one-of-a-kind dental imprint. Even identical twins have different identities! Who, then, can say what's "normal?" Did you know that being left handed was often referred to as "backward writing" and considered to be "abnormal?" Well, Michelangelo painted the entire ceiling of the Sistine Chapel left handed. If the mold was broken after each of us was made, who can say what's normal for you or me?

Divinely Dysfunctional

Holding "irrational beliefs" is another common characteristic given for those who are labeled "dysfunctional." That would make Wilbur and Orville Wright, Sir Isaac Newton, Benjamin Banneker, Thomas Edison, Amelia Earhart, Henry Ford, Mahatma Gandhi, George Washington Carver, Albert Einstein, Nelson Mandela, Galileo Galilei, Harriet Tubman, Plato, Booker T. Washington and Mother Teresa all dysfunctional. Not too shabby a class of dysfunctional people, wouldn't you say?

Another characteristic of a dysfunctional person or family member has to do with fears. A fear of being vulnerable, a fear of success, a fear of failure and a fear of rejection are all considered to be dysfunctional behaviors. But how can this be, since fear is a natural response, not a learned one? You and I were born with a healthy fear. Tests have shown that fear of falling is innate. So, since we were born with fear, does that mean that we were all created "dysfunctional?"

No two people are exactly alike, and too often there is a rush toward oversimplification or categorization, to offer an explanation for that which we don't fully understand. The truth is that we're not dysfunctional, just different.

As Chris Divine spoke, all of the air in the huge auditorium seemed to go out of it and was replaced with thought, doubt, disbelief and some anger. Chris wondered to himself if his concept was being received as new and insightful or with guile and contempt for him daring to question the *status quo*. Either way, he wasn't too worried, because he knew he was speaking from his heart. The psychology of today says that when you speak, you should think about the people you care about. Soften your throat, eyes, chest and heart. Bring to mind what you want to say. Then take another breath and start speaking.

Another rule is to always try to stay in touch with your experience as you express it, and that's exactly what Chris had done and was doing. In fact, his whole series of lectures had been born out of his own family experiences. Over the years he had been told many stories about various members of his family who had one dysfunction or another. But Chris's family members, like the list of notables he shared with the class, were also great people. Chris hoped and believed that by sharing their story, he might be able to help someone else embrace their dysfunction and go on to greatness.

Chris was tall, handsome, well-educated and only in his thirties. The word around campus was that he was from a very prestigious family overseas. Perhaps even royalty, some suggested. He always seemed so quiet and reserved, as if he was constantly in deep thought about something. Although everything on the surface appeared calm, however, you knew he had a past. We all do. He continued his instructive lecture:

Every good thing is not necessarily good for you, and neither is every bad thing bad for you. Sometimes the mixture of both is what we need. For example, think about your vehicle. In order for you to advance on your journey, something positive, as well as something negative, must take place. Both the positive and the negative posts of your car battery are needed to work together, if your vehicle is even to start.

Think of our lives as vehicles by which we journey through time. As with the car battery, both positive and negative occurrences are required to help us move from place to place. If we experienced only good, then we could never move to grow and experience great. If all were bad, then we could never hope for the good. I heard somewhere that the number one enemy of "great" is "good."

Remember what I said, that everyone has a bit of dysfunction in their family? Well, I personally have had more than just a bit. Not only did I have some "normalcy" issues of my own, but my family has a laundry list dating back several decades, and I want to share some of those with you in the days ahead. I can't tell you everything in just one lecture, but over the coming days and weeks, more and more of these truths will emerge.

§

As a young boy, I was always being taunted by other children because of my family situation. It was not easy growing up in West Asia as a child conceived by an unwed teenage mother. I was called "infidel," "bastard child," and "a mistake," among other cruel things. By the time of my birth, Mother had married a good man, but I was still the target of a lot of hateful darts. All too often, someone would say to me jeeringly, "Oh, by the way, Chris, who's your daddy?" There was no answer. Because of it, I never really seemed to fit in anywhere and was always feeling like I was the outsider, the one who didn't belong. Either I was too good for the bad kids or too conscientious for the good ones.

All this seemed to fit the modern psychological profile of children born to teenage mothers. They are, we are told, more likely to have social, health and emotional problems than children born to older mothers. But what if our dysfunction was by design rather than disaster? Maybe I, like Leonardo de Vince, was destined for greatness. As a result of my being a social outcast, I spent a lot of time by myself, and this helped me develop character.

And I wasn't really alone; I had the sheep that roamed the hillside near our humble home to keep me company. This fellowship with the sheep led to something quite different. Often, one of the sheep would get injured, perhaps by a natural predator or in an accident. Either way, I was somehow compelled to come to their aide. I would ever-so-gently approach the wounded animal and lay my hands on them, and this alone seemed to bring them both comfort and healing.

Yes, I said *healing*! It all seemed very miraculous. After I touched an ailing sheep, it would recover its strength and be able to resume its normal activities. I guess you could call me some sort of sheep whisperer.

But, as it turned out, this healing touch worked wonders on some people as well. Once, while I was with the children of our township, one of the boys got hurt. His knee popped out of place. I didn't just pop his knee back into place, as some might have done. Instead, I simply laid my hand on the boy, and he was able to walk away unfazed by his injury.

That was the moment when this illegitimate boy, who often played alone, became known as "Touch." It was said that once I touched something it was restored, and my fame soon spread. I couldn't help everyone, but I did help many.

For the most part, my mother tried to help me have as nearly normal a childhood as could be expected, considering the bad start. She insisted that I try to play with other children, attend classes at school and learn the family trade. With all of this, however, there were always the swirling questions about who my real father was.

My step-father was a good man who was in the furniture business. In that business, he wasn't going to get rich, but he could certainly keep busy, and keeping busy was what I needed. The more time I spent in the shop the better, as far as I was concerned. I was honing my skills for the future, while shaping, molding and putting things together.

I seemed to have a knack for it. Where most people would just see a big stump of a cypress tree, I saw a potentially beautiful chair. The average person would see a pile of useless sticks, but I saw in them a very beautiful table.

Yes, I seemed to have a knack for seeing what no one else could see. No matter how worn or useless others thought some item to be, I insisted that it still had value. I certainly loved restoring things, and people were no different to me. They needed restoration like any inanimate object.

Despite how cruel some folks had been to me and my family, I never gave up on humanity. I believed that people were the most valuable of all resources, and I loved talking to them and hearing their stories. Another new gift was starting to emerge in my life.

§

One summer, when I was twelve, my family decided to take a retreat in a far city with other members of the community, and a road trip sounded to me like a wonderful adventure. And off we went.

When we reached our campsite, the men and women split up, and I was allowed to go with the men. *This was going to be great,* I was thinking to myself, *all these men and all their stories.* One-by-one I listened to each and every one of them. When someone noticed how attentive I was to their conversation, they asked me what I was thinking. I answered, "Wow! What an honor it is to be asked to join in with this great brain-trust!" These were some of the great men of our community and of the surrounding towns.

This seemed to open a valve of some sort, and suddenly I began to talk and to share things that seemed well beyond the knowledge of a twelve-year-old, especially the son of a furniture dealer. The men were amazed, and on and on we talked, for hours on end. Politics, religion, global warming ... I shared my thoughts on all of it.

All the time I had spent by myself pondering such things was starting to pay off. I was beginning to feel almost normal, like I was in the right place doing the right thing, somewhere where I could actually fit in and belong.

I was enjoying it so much that I lost track of the time and wasn't with our group as they broke camp and headed back home. It was only later that Mom suddenly noticed that she hadn't seen her rambunctious boy in a while. *Perhaps he's with the other children who made the trip,* she thought. But that was not likely, she realized. I was something of an odd ball, so she went looking for me.

Mom and my step-dad looked and looked, but I was nowhere to be found. Eventually they decided that I must have been left behind, so they left the group and started backtracking, going back to everywhere they had been, and, as they did, they questioned everyone along the way.

Meanwhile, hours had gone by as I talked with and listened to the elder statesmen of the community. I was having the time of my life ... until I saw my parents standing there looking at me. That was when everything came crashing back to earth. When they had finally found me, I was just sitting there talking with everyone, but they were understandably furious. I had caused them to worry so.

My step-dad was the first to speak, "Where have you been all this time, young man?"

"We've been worried sick about you," my mother chimed in.

And that was where things seemed to go off course. I had not intended to be disrespectful to my parents, and yet, before I knew what I was doing, my mouth opened and I replied, "I was doing exactly what I was created to do."

"Just what do you mean by that?" my step-dad insisted. "Was there some carpentry work or furniture that needed repaired here?"

"No," I told him, "not *your* work, but *His*." And I was pointing toward the sky. It had suddenly dawned on me, not only that I loved reasoning with other people, but also that I was good at it. For their part, my parents just stood and looked at me. No one else seemed to understand what I was saying. How could they?

It was a very quiet trip back home. I didn't want to hurt my parents or bring shame on the family, but I sensed that I had begun to walk in my purpose and was sure that others would understand in time.

Even then, Mom seemed to understand more than anyone else. Whether it was by maternal instinct or divine intervention, she understood that I had been sent to heal and never hurt, to put things back together that had long been torn apart. I desired to do no harm.

The important thing to say, in concluding this lecture, is that I, like the rest of you, survived my childhood and grew to be a young man, one who thought it was better to face his destiny than to try to escape it.

We will continue this theme in our next session. I want you to see that even though some people seem to be dysfunctional, the truth is that they are *Divinely Dysfunctional.*

CHAPTER 2

A BEAUTIFUL CODEPENDENCY

*A bad day can happen anytime
you don't focus on the good.*

*P*rofessor Jones again opens the class. "As you know, class, we have been enjoying the unique perspective of a guest lecturer, renowned in his field, Dr. Christopher Divine. I'm sure you have found his words both challenging and enlightening. Now, without any further ado, let's welcome him to continue his theme, "Good Dysfunction."

Good morning. Let me continue where we left off with the last class. Because of my upbringing, I was always the type of person others felt like they could talk to about anything. One day a lady walked right up to me, started sharing with me her life story and then asked me what I thought she should do about her situation.

This woman told me that she was tired of being alone and didn't want to spend the rest of her life by herself. "I'm reasonably attractive," she said, "and in good health. I'm also a good cook, and I'm not afraid of hard work. I don't know why I can't seem to find Mr. Right."

I have found that it is a waste of people's time to beat around the bush, so I answered her directly and forcefully: "You're the problem."

This surprised her. "I'm the problem?" she asked. "How am I the problem?"

"Well, you've sold yourself too cheap," I said. "You really don't think all that highly of yourself, and that's why, in the past, you've been willing to settle for anyone who would pay you any attention at all."

Divinely Dysfunctional

I was sure I was onto something that would help the woman, so I continued. "How many times have you been married? What's it been ... three or more times? If the truth were to be told, you probably have some guy living with you right now who really doesn't care anything about you. Just because he noticed you, you were willing to give him a try. Isn't that right?"

With her head bowed and tears running down her face, the woman confessed, "Your right, but how do I change things?"

That's always an important question, and I had the answer. "You've got to start believing in your own self-worth," I said. "You're a one-of-a-kind creation. God never made another person like you. Sure, there might be someone who looks similar, but their fingerprints are different. That makes you a one-of-a-kind creation." I could see that she was listening intently.

"Anyone will tell you that a one-of-a-kind of anything is very valuable," I continued. "You have to see yourself as a valuable person. Once you begin to do this, then you will quit settling for whatever comes along. When something settles, it's always at the bottom. Aren't you tired of picking from the bottom?"

As I tried to encourage the woman to increase her self-esteem, my thoughts went to one of the many strong women in our family, a distant relative of mine named Jan.

Jan was a classic example of a very self-confident woman who was unwilling to settle, and the result was that she became a matriarch in the family. Her story is both sad and informative.

§

Jan and her husband Lem, along with their two boys, Mace and Chase, were forced from their home by some very harsh economic times. Lem thought it best for the family to relocate to another country to the south, where they heard things were better. They packed up everything they had and moved. This was considered to be a very radical thing to do at the time, to become immigrants to a strange land, but Lem was willing to take the risk to feed his family.

It was tough going for the young couple with two small children, but Lem was willing to accept any work anywhere he could get it. He worked long hours and was rarely at home.

Divinely Dysfunctional

This left Jan with the task of parenting the two boys herself. Days went by when it was just her and the boys, trying to make it the best way they knew how.

One day, when the sons had grown into teenagers, they and Jan were sitting around the house talking when there came a knock at the door. Since they rarely had visitors, whenever there was such a knock Jan always feared the worst. This time she was right. This visitor had come with news that Jan's husband, the boys' father, had died.

Oh, my! What was Jan going to do now? She had no family nearby, no friends to speak of, and no real skills, so the outlook for the future of her little family was bleak. As she sat with her teenage sons and broke the tragic news to them, the consensus was that they should go back home. But how? The boys decided to get jobs and earn money so that the family could travel.

Like their father, Mace and Chase were both good workers, and, for a time, everything seemed to go well for them. Their work was steady, and so the household was stabilized. In the meantime, the boys both met local girls and decided to settle down and marry. Mace married a girl named Olive, and Chase married a girl named Rue.

Olive's parents weren't too thrilled about the idea of their daughter being in a mixed marriage, but they soon accepted it. As for Rue, she was adopted, so her family's transition was a little easier. Even though there were cultural differences between the men and their wives, they all seemed to get along fine, and both families managed to live together peacefully under Jan's roof.

Jan and her daughters-in-law grew close, until they all formed one big happy family. The wives would often sit and talk with their mother-in-law about her childhood in the old country. Jan, which means "sweetness," began to feel a little better about how things in her life were turning out. Then, as the women were making preparations for dinner one night, they were interrupted by a knock at the door. Jan froze right where she was, and it was Olive who went to answer the door.

Jan was right to be concerned. Once again death had knocked at her door. This time the tragic news was that both of her sons had been killed. She slumped to the floor and wept bitterly.

Divinely Dysfunctional

"Why, God? Why? What have I done to have so much tragedy in my life? My life hasn't been a ray of sunshine; it's been a storm."

Jan was so depressed that she stayed in bed for the next few days, refusing both food and company. When she finally addressed her grieving daughters-in-law, it was to inform them of her decision to go back to her homeland. Both of them replied, without hesitation, that they would go with her.

"Why?" Jan asked. "I have no more sons to offer you for husbands? What would you do with only an old woman for company? You would both be better off staying here in your own country. Maybe you can find someone else and remarry. As for me, I'm too old, and even if I did remarry and have more sons, it would be years before they were old enough to marry you. Why waste all that time?"

Still, Jan's two daughters-in-law insisted that they would rather go with her. After more tears and unsuccessful pleading, she kissed the women good-bye. She told Olive to return to her mother and to allow herself some time to heal, and Olive obediently departed.

Next, Jan turned to Rue and said, "You, too, must go to your mother."

Rue answered, "You are my mother, and I will go wherever you go. I will never leave your side. I vow to be with you until the end of time. You will never be alone again. Your people will be my people, your faith will be my faith, and I will be right beside you when you take your last breath. All that we know is what *has* happened. Now let us see what *will* happen."

So, Jan and Rue set out together for the long journey back to Jan's homeland. Along the way, the women received news that the economy in Jan's native land had recovered and was booming once again. Another excellent bit of news was that many agricultural workers were being sought in the particular town that Jan was from. That sounded good to the women.

When they reached the city limits, many people came out to greet them. The news of their return had traveled fast, and old friends were delighted to see Jan and to welcome her daughter-in-law. Strangely, Jan did not seem like her old self. She was withdrawn and short with her friends. "Why do you come to see an old, broken-down widow woman, whose family is all dead?" she said. "It's obvious that God has cursed me. Stand clear, or you, too, might be cursed."

Taking into account the tragic losses Jan had suffered, her friends decided to give her time to settle in and grieve sufficiently. She would surely come around.

The women had returned just at the beginning of the harvest season, and now they had to figure out how they would support themselves. "Momma," Rue said, "don't worry about a thing. I'm young and strong, and I can get a job as a laborer in the fields."

So they begin to inquire as to who was hiring and what the going wages were. Someone mentioned that one of Jan's distant relatives, a man named Bo Kingsley, was doing quite well for himself. He now owned many properties and always needed more workers. They decided to go see for themselves.

It was all true. Bo Kingsley was a good businessman. When the land had been cheap, because of the drought, he had bought up as much of it as he could. Then he bided his time until the weather had turned and was good again for planting. He had planted, and his big investment was now paying off.

After surveying the Kingsley lands, Rue turned to her mother-in-law and said, "It's settled then. I'll go and apply for a job tomorrow. It certainly can't hurt my chances when he finds out that I'm the daughter-in-law of one of his relatives."

"You have been such a dear daughter to me," Jan said. "Yes, go and see what the future holds."

The next morning Rue arrived at the Kingsley fields early to seek employment. She was hired on the spot and asked to begin work immediately. She was excited and thrilled and gave thanks to God. This was exactly the new beginning she and Jan so desperately needed. She purposed in her heart to be one of the hardest workers around, and she set to work with a song in her heart.

The work was not easy, in any sense of the word. Before long, with the sun beaming brightly on her, both of Rue's hands and even her hair were covered in dirt, but she was still smiling joyfully. "Why are you so happy?" a voice behind her asked.

Divinely Dysfunctional

Placing one hand over her eyes to shade them from the sun, Rue saw a gentleman standing nearby. "I'm just glad to have a job," she answered.

"Well, I've been watching you," the man said, "and you're one of the best workers we have."

This pleased Rue and she smiled and answered, "Good! That was my goal."

"Well, good day," the man said, "perhaps we'll talk again soon." And he turned and ambled away.

Mr. Kingsley hadn't gone far when he encountered one of his field supervisors. "Who is that woman?" he asked, pointing toward Rue.

"Why, Mr. Kingsley," the supervisor said, "that's your relative, Jan's daughter-in-law. When she came in today seeking employment, I immediately put her to work because I thought we could use the help. Is there something wrong with her?"

"Nothing at all," Bo answered with a smile. "In fact, she seems to be one of our best workers. Make sure you afford her every courtesy that the veteran laborers deserve, including regular break periods from the hot sun, and allow her time to refresh herself with water from the well."

"Yes, sir, Mr. Kingsley," the field supervisor answered.

Bo then turned away from the man and walked back to where Rue was working. "Excuse me again, young lady," he said. "I'd like to introduce myself. I'm Bo Kingsley, and this is my field that you're working in. I just wanted to tell you that I appreciate the work you're doing and have instructed my men to treat you as a senior employee. I assure you no one will harass you when you take a break to refresh yourself at the well."

Rue couldn't believe her good fortune. Overwhelmed with gratitude, she fell at the man's feet, thanking him for the job and for the kindness he had shown her.

"As a matter of fact," Bo continued, "I'm about to take lunch now. Would you care to join me?"

"Oh, yes," Rue said excitedly.

So off they went together to Bo's house to share a meal.

When they got to the house, Rue couldn't believe what she was seeing. People were everywhere, and they were all deeply respectful of her new boss. Still, all of them seemed to be enjoying themselves. When servants brought Bo and Rue their meals, it was not with sorrow or fearfulness. They were very relaxed and polite.

As they ate, Bo told Rue how wonderful he thought it was for her to care for her mother-in-law the way she had. He also expressed his condolences for the loss of her husband and father-in-law. "Furthermore," he said, "consider yourself now to be a full-time worker with us. We need more hard-working people like you around here."

When Rue was leaving to go back to the field, Bo motioned for a supervisor to come to him. He told the man to be sure to give a healthy bonus to this young woman for her hard work that day and to do it every day going forward. The supervisor did as he had been instructed.

Rue couldn't wait until the end of the day when she could go home and share the good news with Jan. She ran into the house and said, "Momma, guess what? You will never guess what happened today."

"What is it, child?" Jan asked.

Rue could barely contain herself as she shared the events of the day. "I got there early this morning, just like you told me. I spoke with a field supervisor, and he asked me if I could begin work immediately. The harvest is huge and so ready for reaping. Of course I agreed and took off running toward the field he indicated, ready to work."

Jan was visibly pleased with this news and encouraged her daughter-in-law to continue.

"Well," Rue said, "there I was, just working and smiling to myself, thanking God for our new start, when a gentleman approached and asked me why I was so happy. I told him that I was just glad to be working, and he walked away. But, then, a little while later, he came back to where I was working and started talking to me some more. He said that I was a good worker, and he even invited me to have lunch with him."

"Who was this man?" Jan asked.

"That's the best part, Momma," Rue answered. "It was the owner, your relative, Bo Kingsley. As I was leaving to go back to work, I overheard him telling a supervisor to give me a bonus, since I had worked so hard. And not only today, but for every day I work I'll receive a bonus. Isn't that great news?"

Jan's smile broadened, and she said, "Maybe God is shining His favor on us after all, dear daughter."

Soon the two of them went to the market with the wages from that day, and all the way there and back, Rue continued to talk about how kind Bo had been to her. "Sounds like you're as attracted to him as he seems to be to you," Jan said.

Rue just smiled and said, "He is quite handsome, and awfully kind and generous."

"Don't forget wealthy," Jan said.

"That's true," said Rue. "They say he's been a very savvy businessman."

Days and weeks passed, and Rue continued to work just as hard as she had that first day. From time to time, Bo would stop by and invite her to lunch with him, and every day ended with her receiving a bonus for her efforts in the field that day. But now the end of the harvest season was approaching.

As was customary in those days, each landholder would store in barns all the grain that wasn't immediately used or sold, to be used as seed for the following year. It was a most valuable commodity. That night, the women were sitting together in the house, and Jan said, "When do you intend to let him know how you feel?"

"Who?" Rue asked.

"Why, Bo, of course!" Jan said with a sly smile and, looking Rue right in the eyes continued, "Daughter, when do you plan to let him know you're in love with him? Do you think he'll wait forever? You're not getting any younger, and neither is he. I believe he's already about ten or so years your senior."

Rue's face revealed that Jan was right about her being in love with her boss. But she shrugged her shoulders and said, "I'm not quite sure how to approach him. I don't want to ruin a good thing and jeopardize our income."

"Well, let me tell you what to do," Jan said. "Tonight is a perfect night to let him know how you feel. He'll be at the barn late like all the other landowners, preparing for the off season. Don't lose another day."

Rue leaned toward her mother-in-law and listened intently to what the woman was saying. "Listen carefully now," Jan continued. "You should get a nice bath, spray on a soft fragrance, put on some relaxing, yet sexy, clothes and then march yourself right up to that barn tonight."

Jan had Rue's attention, so she added, "Wait until it's late, and Bo's tired from his long day of work. Then go in and offer to give him a massage. Once you've done all that, then tell him how you feel."

The thought of it thrilled Rue, and she paused only a moment before saying, "All right, Momma, I'll do just as you say." And with that she went to bathe and ready herself to go up to the barn to meet Bo.

When Rue arrived at the barn, Bo was already asleep on a bed set up in the middle of a large room. At first she felt awkward and started to leave, but something told her it would be all right to stay. She decided to sit down on the foot of the bed and wait until Bo awoke. After a while she, too, became sleepy, lay down and fell sound asleep.

Late in the night Bo woke up and was frightened to find someone in bed with him. "Who are you?" he asked, "and what are you doing here?"

"It's me, Rue," she answered. "I came to see if you wanted a massage because I knew you would be working late."

"Is that all?" Bo prodded.

"Well, no," she admitted, "I wanted to let you know how much I appreciate the kindness and care you have shown me."

"I'm only glad to do it," Bo said.

Smiling broadly, Rue went on, slow at first, "Also ... I wanted to let you know that I would love to spend more time with you during this off-season."

"I'm flattered," Bo responded. "I know there are many men, both young and old, who would love to have attention from someone as beautiful as you." Then, without warning, he leaned forward and kissed her. "I've been drawn to you since the first time I laid eyes on you," he said, "and being here with you tonight is like a dream come true."

"It is for me too," she agreed.

Emboldened now, Bo continued, "I would love to take you as my wife. The only thing stopping me from asking you tonight is our custom of speaking with Jan's oldest male relative, to ask permission for her daughter's hand in marriage. Even though you are her daughter-in-law, you're still under her authority. In order for me to be honorable to both you and her, I must ask first. If you'll give me until tomorrow to check with him, then I'd love for us to have dinner tomorrow night and we'll talk about it."

"Tomorrow will be fine," Rue said, now glowing.

"One more thing before you go," Bo added. "Take my family medallion as proof of my intentions to ask you to marry me." Rue took the medallion and went merrily on her way home.

The next morning Jan was very excited to hear how the night had gone. When Rue told her what had been said and done, Jan said, "Let's wait and see what happens 'the morning after,' just as you have said, dear daughter."

True to his word, Bo went and spoke with the elder relative of Jan, and that relative had no objections to Bo's proposal for Jan's daughter-in-law. Others in the family were asked to witness this approval so there would be no question of honor later. Together, the family members wished Bo and Rue all the joy in the world and prayed that God would bless them with great children. Since all agreed, the matter was settled, and now all Bo had to do was ask Rue for her hand in marriage.

Later that evening, at dinner, Bo did just that. Rue happily accepted, and they soon married.

Just as the family members had prayed, Rue soon became pregnant and bore Bo a wonderful son, whom they named Ovell. Rue was excited about being a mother, and Jan was excited about being a grandmother. She thanked God for His faithfulness to her through this entire ordeal.

But God hadn't finish showering Rue or Jan with blessings. Their bloodline produced many great leaders, one of whom became a king. All of this happened to two unlikely women. One of them was getting up in age and thought she had been cursed by God. The other was perhaps considered by some to be a seductive gold digger. Only God knows the end of a matter and what is in a person's heart. I'm sure some thought them to be dysfunctional, but the truth is that they were both *Divinely Dysfunctional*.

CHAPTER 3

A BLESSED BORDELLO

Honor isn't a medal, it's a responsibility.

gain Professor Jones does the honors of introducing the guest lecturer to the class, and the next lecture begins:

In the last session, I told you about my relatives Rue and Jan and their sketchy background. There was another strong woman in my background, and her story is even more unusual. She was Bo's mother, and her name was Rhoby.

When Bo was so kind to Rue, it may have been because his own family was no stranger to scandal and controversy. It's true what they say about everybody having a story to tell, and Rhoby's was quite a story indeed.

§

Like so many of every generation, Rhoby was no stranger to the struggles of life. Her parents worked hard to support five children in a war-torn community. But even within her own household, she had challenges. With two older sisters and two younger brothers, Rhoby was the dreaded middle child, you know, the one who never seems to fit in anywhere. Everything was: "Why can't you be more like your older sisters" or "Quit acting like a kid with your baby brothers." It was hard being the middle child.

Rumor had it that, after two girls, Rhoby's father wanted a son so bad that he declared,

Divinely Dysfunctional

"The next child born in this family will be named Rhoby." True to his word, he named her Rhoby, not Robin or Roberta. Rhoby was kind of an odd name for a girl, but she just went with it. Sometimes, when you receive lemons, you just have to try and make some lemonade.

It might have been the name that gave Rhoby her somewhat fearless nature. She wasn't all that good in school, had only a few friends, and it was no picnic being a military officer's kid. People seem to expect more from you when you're from a military family, especially a general. Well, Rhoby's father wasn't really a general, but he might as well have been because of the strict code of conduct he set for his children. There were so many rules and regulations, and none of the children ever seemed to do anything right. At least that was Rhoby's perspective. Because of this, when she was old enough to move out on her own, she did just that.

Life on her own was more demanding than Rhoby had imagined. Between her rent, other responsibilities and food, making ends meet was always a task, and there weren't that many job opportunities available for a female civilian in a military town. One day a friend who knew that Rhoby was looking for work told her about a lady who was hiring young women. The friend didn't really know what the ladies would be doing, but she heard that the pay was great. Roby thanked her for the tip and immediately set out to find the lady in question and ask her for a job. She had become desperate.

When Rhoby arrived at the lady's house, she quickly learned that the job opening she had heard about for young ladies was for prostitution. That certainly wasn't her first choice, but she sure could use the money right about then. Of course, working as a prostitute meant that she would be estranged from her family. There was no way her military father would ever approve of having his daughter be a prostitute. Reluctantly she accepted the job. She didn't know what else to do.

After many weeks in her new position, Rhoby was finally doing well enough to adequately support herself. From time to time, she would hear from her mother and siblings, but never a word from her dad.

Then, one afternoon, Rhoby heard some disturbing news. A foreign army was fast approaching the town from the west. All soldiers in the town were put on full alert, and everyone was told to stay in their homes.

Rhoby lived on the outskirts of town, in a small house near the wall that surrounded the city. Upon hearing this news, she rushed home to prepare for whatever was coming. Few know the rigors of war like those who have lived in or near a military community. Rhoby had no idea what to expect.

While she was no stranger to the ills of war, Rhoby had never known what it was like to have her own town placed under siege. After searching her house carefully for any unwelcome visitors, she curled up in the corner with a blanket and just sat there ever so quietly.

Before long, it seemed like she had been hiding there for hours or days (when, in actuality, it was probably just a matter of minutes). *This is silly,* she thought to herself. *I'm not about to feel like a prisoner in my own home.* She got up and began to move about.

Before long, there was a knock at Rhoby's door. Very cautiously she proceeded to see who it was. When she opened the door, two strange men stood there looking at her. One of them had been injured.

"Sorry to bother you so late, miss," the other man said. "My friend and I were traveling near here when he injured his leg. Then we saw your light on and decided to stop for help. Can you help us?"

"We've all been told to stay in our homes," she told them, " because we are under a military alert. Didn't you notice the guards patrolling the streets?"

"We didn't see anyone on the way we came in," the man answered.

About that time his companion collapsed. "Please, miss, will you help us?" he pleaded.

Rhoby was hesitant, but she couldn't just let the man bleed to death. Reluctantly she said, "Well, bring him in and let him rest over there on the couch. I'll let you spend the night, but you must leave in the morning."

Before the man could get his friend inside and settled, she decoded to question him more: "Where did you say you were from? And where exactly was it that you were you heading?"

"Please, miss," he pleaded very politely, "I'll be glad to answer all your questions, but let me get my friend inside and cared for. Do you have anything I could use to bandage his leg?"

"At least tell me your name," she insisted.

"Oh, forgive me, miss," he said, "my name is Saulizar, but they call me Sal."

"Hi, Sal," she said, "I'm Rhoby. What's your friend's name?"

"Jerry," he told her.

As Sal focused on tending to Jerry's wounded leg, Rhoby continued to make small talk. "Tell me the truth. You really aren't travelers, are you? You're army scouts, right?"

"It's true," Sal said. "Please don't turn us in."

"Why shouldn't I?" she insisted.

"Because," he said, "if we don't return to our camp safely, our army will attack and destroy your whole town."

Rhoby thought for a moment. "Well, what do I get for helping you?" she asked.

Sal explained that he wasn't in a position to cut deals, but he was willing to listen to her proposals.

"If I turn you in now," she said, "they'll kill you both long before your army will ever be able to get here. What I'm suggesting is a fair and even exchange—your lives in return for the lives of me and my family."

"I've heard that your people are very gracious," Rhoby continued. "Isn't it true that you believe that your god has shown you favor and will favor all those who help you?" Rhoby knew that this was a gamble, but she had to take it. If this enemy army invaded, her family would be imprisoned or worse because her father was a military man.

After thinking on her proposal, Sal said, "I'll tell my commanding officer how you have helped us, and I'm sure he'll be grateful."

"Grateful?" she said rather scornfully. "What does '*grateful*' mean? I'm not asking for gratitude. Either you allow me and my family to go free, or I will report you to my people. Now, do we have a deal or not?"

Sal was impressed with this woman's pluck. Smiling he asked, "Has anyone ever said 'no' to you, Miss Rhoby?"

"Not lately," Rhoby said.

"Well, then, I won't break the trend," Sal answered. "Yes, we have a deal."

Divinely Dysfunctional

They must have talked a great part of the night, and then, as the sun was coming up the next morning, Rhoby told the men that they should move up to the attic and stay there until she signaled that the coast was clear. While Sal moved Jerry upstairs, she cleaned up the blood in the room and got rid of any other sign of her visitors.

Rhoby finished this none too soon, for someone was suddenly knocking loudly on her door. When she opened it, three local soldiers rushed in. They immediately began to question her about whether or not she had seen two men who were suspected of being spies. She denied seeing any spies, and, quickly changing the subject, told them that most of her clients were soldiers just like them. "Would you boys care to stay a while so we could have some fun?" she suggested. *If I pretend to be open for business*, she was thinking, *they'll accept that I was home alone and leave.*

"Maybe later," one of the men said. "Right now we're on high alert," and they all three turned and headed for the door.

Rhoby breathed a sign of relief. Her plan had worked to perfection. As soon as the soldiers were out of sight, she rushed to the attic to tell

Sal what had happened and recommend that he and Jerry leave before the soldiers could return. She told them about a hunting cabin her father had in the mountains and suggested that they hide out there for a while before returning to their camp, since soldiers would be scouring the countryside looking for them. Sal thanked her for her help and vowed to keep his word concerning her family's safety.

"I've kept my end of the bargain," Rhoby said. "Now how do I know that you'll keep yours? And how will your army know my family from all the others?"

Sal quickly came up with a plan: Rhoby must make sure that all of her family members were with her in her home during the coming invasion, and she must wrap her window with a piece of scarlet thread. It would be a sign to let the men of his army know that this was the house of the woman who had so graciously helped them.

Inquisitive, Rhoby asked, "Why a scarlet thread?"

Sal explained to her that, to his people, scarlet represented the shed blood of one who had sacrificed his life for another's. Satisfied, Rhoby led them to a place behind her house where they could scale the wall without being detected. Both men thanked her again and quickly fled to safety.

Later that day, Rhoby went to her parents' house and told her family what had happened. Although her father wasn't pleased that she had risked her life in this way, he commended her for such an act of bravery, and then they rushed to get everyone to Rhoby's house.

By the time they all got settled, the first incoming waves of attack were taking place. Little by little, the invading army devastated the town and its buildings, but Rhoby's home was spared. Sal had been true to his word and had kept his vow to her.

A few days later, things had quieted down enough that Rhoby dared to open her front door so that they could all survey the damage firsthand. Much to her surprise, she saw Sal coming up the street. When he saw her, they both just stood there looking at each other for a moment. Then, smiling broadly, he said, "I trust that you and your family are well."

"Yes,"she answered, "as a matter of fact, we are," and she returned his broad smile.

It was at that moment in time that the two of them realized that theirs had been no chance meeting but rather a divine appointment. Sal soon asked Rhoby to marry him and go back to his country with him once the war was over. She gladly accepted and began to make preparations for the journey.

Leaving a place and a people she had known all her life was hard for Rhoby, but she felt that she was doing the right thing. Understandably, her mom and siblings all had mixed feelings about her proposed marriage to someone outside their race, but they were hopeful for her happiness.

Rhoby's father eventually came around as well. He and Rhoby were actually able to have a conversation and to discuss things, at which point he told her how proud he was of her. Everyone was hopeful for their future. So Rhoby and her husband-to-be set out on their journey together.

Sal was very excited for Rhoby to meet his family and friends. As soon as they arrived in his homeland, word began to spread about the soldier who had married the prostitute. She had not only saved his life; she had also aided the army in their victory. In this way, Rhoby became an instant folk hero and, for the first time in her life, felt that she was in a place where she actually fit in. She was grateful to God for her new life.

The newlyweds were landowners and farmers, like so many others in that region, and it wasn't long before she became pregnant. Both she and Sal began to plan for their family.

Sal, of course, wanted a boy, but Rhoby's only request was that the child be healthy. She vowed to love their child immeasurably—whether it was a boy or a girl.

Everyone seemed pleased when Rhoby gave birth to a bouncing baby boy (whom they named Bo). Only God could have envisioned the end of a prostitute's life turning out so wonderfully, but she was clearly *Divinely Dysfunctional*."

CHAPTER 4

A BURNING SINSATION

*It's not about what you did, but
rather what you undid.*

*C*hris was again introduced by Professor Jones and began his next lecture.

Good morning. My life as a healthcare physician has been very demanding, as you can imagine, but because of the way I grew up, I somehow always find time for children. It doesn't matter if I know them or not, and no matter what I am doing or where I happen to be, if a child wants to talk with me, I will stop right where I am and what I am doing and give them an audience. I feel very deeply that children, regardless of their history, are inherently honest and forthright.

Notice that I said "inherently." We must take into account the fact that we all pick up various behavioral patterns from the world around us. Often children (as well as adults) are invited to partake in situations that have ramifications far beyond the point their imagination can take them. Those experiences can be either good or bad, depending on the inviter. That's why I always feel an urgency to listen to the hearts of children. My hope is that perhaps I can help them to become better informed, so that they can then make better choices in life. In reality, each of us could use someone offering up insights to aide us in seeing the whole picture.

Divinely Dysfunctional

Think of a book, if you will. Notice how, when it is closed, you can see that a book has a front cover, back cover, spine and three views of the pages. A book, then, has six different surfaces or planes, and each has its own viewpoint. But I think it fair to say that, at any given time, the most viewpoints you could possibly see of it would be three.

Much in our lives is like this book. At most we can only see three viewpoints at any one time. Sometimes we see much less than that, but assuredly it is never more than three perspectives.

The six viewpoints I mentioned don't include opening the book. When you do that, you have to add new perspectives, considering the depth and volume of the contents. This brings me to the conclusion that there is no possible way I can see all sides of my life from my own perspective. Trying to do that without the trusting eyes of others could prove to be a very costly and, quite possibly, dangerous experiment. Bear with me, and I'll show you where I am going with this.

When I was born, even though it was to a teenage mother, many wanted to proclaim me as king. That seemed to be a stretch, but I did have royalty in my bloodline in generations past. His name was King Darren, and he was someone who surely could have used the eyes of others to help him see the whole picture. Having more eyes at work could have helped him avoid some very costly mistakes.

§

As the story goes, Darren's reign came during a time of war, and the country was divided. Civil unrest was everywhere you turned. When Darren's great test came, all of his chief advisors and generals were off at the battlefront with the soldiers, and he had only a handful of staff that had stayed back at the palace with him.

To King Darren, it seemed like months had passed with no word from the front, when, in fact, it was probably just a few weeks. Whatever the length of time, boredom was quickly setting in, and the king was getting cabin fever. You may have heard the saying, "Heavy is the head that wears the crown." This was true of Darren.

One night, while working through one of his regular bouts with insomnia, Darren decided to take a stroll out on his balcony. It was a clear night, with not a cloud in the sky, the kind of night in which it seems like you can see far beyond this galaxy and deep into the next. Darren's thoughts were not nearly as far away as that. He could not help but wonder what was happening just across the horizon. Were his soldiers being defeated? Or were they standing strong in victory? His future and the future of his nation and people depended on it.

The moon was shining so bright that night that it was like a spotlight, lighting up every inch of the ground around him. As his eyes continued to scan the landscape, they fell upon something that made him forget all about war for a moment. There, in the moonlit night, was a beautiful young woman openly bathing in her courtyard. He had the perfect vantage point from which to observe her without being noticed, since the palace balcony stood towering above the rest of the city, and so he watched as she thoroughly washed and enjoyed her bath. For her part, surely the woman had no idea that her nudity act was on full display before a royal audience.

After watching for a while, Darren called for a servant to disclose to him the mystery woman's identity. The servant told him that the woman's name was Shelby and that her husband was a lieutenant in the army by the name of Eurie.

"Who is this Eurie?" The king asked. His servant told him that Eurie was a part of the elite Delta Force called The Thirty. Darren immediately knew that this woman was forbidden fruit, but feeling like he just had to get a closer look, he asked the servant to go and bring the woman to his chambers.

This is where Darren could have used another set of eyes, to help him to gain a better perspective on the vastness of the ultimate consequences of his actions. We, too, often make rash decisions without considering the ramifications of having a free will. In short, what will it cost me to do what I want to do? Unfortunately for Darren, he was given no such insight at this moment of weakness.

Shelby was, quite naturally, surprised by being summoned so late in the evening to come to the palace, but she obeyed. After all, it was her king who was requiring her attendance. The two of them sat and talked for a bit, before passion filled the air. Then they engaged in lovemaking, without any regard for their spouses. Afterward,

Divinely Dysfunctional

Shelby gathered her things and was secretly escorted back to her home before daylight.

Days and weeks passed without contact between them, and it seemed that their night of passion might slip into time and be remembered as just a temporary lapse of judgment. Then one day Darren received a message from Shelby, requesting a meeting. He thought it best that they meet in a private location, far from the eyes of others. So they did.

At their meeting, Shelby notified Darren that she had missed her monthly cycle and that she was, therefore, pregnant with his child. Upon hearing this most unsuspected news, Darren was shaken. But he was the king. He had to show strength.

Darren told Shelby just to return home and not worry. He would find a suitable resolution to their situation.

After mulling over this matter in his mind, Darren came up with a plan he thought might work. He would call Lt. Eurie's troop home on leave. He was sure that, after being away for months, Eurie would certainly sleep with his wife, and the pregnancy would be thought to be of their union. He immediately sent word to his friend, General Joseph, to bring the Delta Force home for a debriefing and a first-hand report on the battle.

When the soldiers got back to town, the king immediately sent an order for all of them to go home to their families and rest. He would see them the next day. Each soldier was given a generous supply of food and alcohol to enjoy while on leave.

The next morning Darren sent for his friend, the general, to meet with him in his quarters. After being brought up to speed on the state of the war, Darren began to tell his buddy Joe what he had done. When he got to the part of his plan concerning Eurie sleeping with his wife, Joe stopped him. "That's a problem," Joe said. "I passed Lt. Eurie in the barracks this morning, and he said he had been there all night. He refused to go home."

Upon hearing this, Darren was both upset and unnerved. He told Joe to go and get Lt. Eurie and bring him to the palace. When they returned, the king commended Lt. Eurie on his service and asked him how he was enjoying his leave. Lt. Eurie responded, "I haven't taken any leave or even seen my wife because I was too busy strategizing how we can end the war sooner and come home for good. Besides, there are others to be considered who are still out there fighting and giving their life for my freedom. How could I be so selfish as to think of my own personal desires at a time like this?" In that moment, the man who seemed the least noble of the two was being the most noble. All the king could do was thank Eurie for his services and release him to be on his way.

As he continued to think on the situation, Darren made another bad decision. Rather than face the music, he decided that Eurie must become another victim, to be crushed by the dreaded beast of war. A devious plan was hatched to kill this honorable soldier, husband and patriot. Darren told Joe to redeploy with these troops and head straight into the teeth of the battle. Once in direct contact with the enemy, he was to order Lt. Eurie to lead an attack. Then the general and a few of his men were to fall back, leaving Lt. Eurie and his men unprotected, thus sealing their fate. Sadly, all that King Darren desired he got, but the question remained: was he ready to pay for it?

News of the battle reached the king, and he was told of the deaths of many of his soldiers, including that of Lt. Eurie. He was secretly relieved.

Upon hearing the news of her husband's death, Shelby mourned greatly. She had no knowledge of all the cynical planning that had been going on behind her back. For the remaining months of her pregnancy, she stayed to herself. Then, before the child's birth, Darren took Shelby as another wife so the baby would be born in the palace.

These actions of the king didn't receive a very high approval rating among his followers, but most were afraid to speak out against him. That is … except for a priest who came to the king and told him that God was displeased at what he had done. He warned Darren that the greater the person the greater the accountability.

The day finally arrived, and Shelby gave birth to a baby boy, but there were complications. The best doctors were called in to try and save the child, but to no avail. He died, being only seven days old.

Divinely Dysfunctional

This event was hard on Darren, but it was even harder on Shelby. She slipped into a state of deep depression, now having lost both husband and child in a matter of months. Finally Darren repented, recognizing that the past few months' events were all because of his selfishness, and he vowed to make it up to Shelby.

Shelby became pregnant again, but this time with wonderful results. She gave birth to a healthy, handsome boy whom they named Wiz. Darren vowed to Shelby that this son of theirs would become the next king.

As Wiz grew, people everywhere noticed the great wisdom he had been given. Darren had other sons who were older than Wiz, but this child of Shelby remained his favorite.

Years passed without much incidence, and the king was growing older. Darren's oldest son, Aden, was preparing himself to become king. He was determined to rid his family of those infidels—Shelby and Wiz. Through the years his hatred had grown for his younger (and wiser) step-brother. The king's chief advisors urged that he name Aden as his successor before his health declined any further.

As these discussions were taking place in the king's chambers, Shelby had a visit from the priest who had spoken with Darren when she was pregnant the first time. The priest told her that her life, as well as that of her son, was in danger because of Aden, who was plotting to become the next king. He advised her to speak with the king concerning his vow to make Wiz the next king. Shelby thanked him for his helpful insight and went immediately to speak with Darren.

When Shelby arrived to speak with Darren, he was lying in bed, looking very much like a man ready to die. She told him that Aden was preparing for his coronation as the next king, and she reminded him of his vow to her and before God to name her son Wiz the next king. Darren assured her that he would keep that vow, even on his death bed.

Now Darren sent for his advisors and ordered them to put out an immediate decree, letting everyone in the kingdom know that he was naming Wiz as his successor to the throne. There was to be a big celebration in honor of the new king.

Afterward, Darren spoke with Wiz and told him to rule with the wisdom he had been given. Darren then prayed over his son, the new king, and soon closed his eyes for the final time.

Divinely Dysfunctional

King Wiz ruled well for many years, and his wisdom was so renowned that dignitaries from several neighboring countries sought his counsel. He was a great king. In this way, what had begun as a selfish and tragic lapse in judgment, leading to the death of many, ended as a story of hope and restoration for a woman, her son and a nation.

Who would have ever guessed that this woman, who first appeared on the scene like a stripper, would have married into royalty and given birth to a king? This story reveals two key truths:

1. The first is that any situation can be turned around, no matter how horrific its start, because God is so merciful.

2. The second is that once we repent and decide to begin to make better choices, we can expect to get better results. It's not over till it's over.

King Darren and his illegitimate son may have seemed to many to be dysfunctional. The truth is that they were *Divinely Dysfunctional*.

CHAPTER 5

TWINCEST

If at first you don't succeed, remember:
no one else did either.

rofessor Jones stands at the podium. "I'm sure that you are enjoying these lectures by Dr. Divine as much as I am. Talk about wisdom! He has it. Here he is again."

Thank you, Professor Jones, and good morning, everyone. Have you noticed that everyone seems to think their life is the worst one ever, that nobody has it as bad as they do? There is an old saying that goes like this: "Don't criticize me until you've walked a mile in my shoes." Truer words were never spoken. Sure people have problems. We all do, but this next story is a real doozy.

I remember someone telling me the story, when I was young, of one of my ancestors named Ed. Not long after Ed got married, he suddenly died. Of course the rumor mill put out the story that he had been so mean to his wife that God killed him, but no one really knew what had happened.

After Ed died, his widow slept with her father-in-law and became pregnant with twin boys. Anyway you slice it, that would make her children's father their grandfather as well. It all sounds like something you'd see in a tabloid while you're waiting in line at a grocery store, but much to my chagrin, I learned that every word of it was true. *Now that was a really close-knit family,* I thought to myself, and I inquired among my relatives as to how this real-life soap opera had played out.

Divinely Dysfunctional

Everyone always talked about my great-great-great-great Uncle Abe, how he was such a wonderful, God-fearing man and a millionaire to boot. "Don't tell me this scandal involved good ole uncle Abe!" I said.

"Not this one," I was told, "although Uncle Abe did have a few skeletons in his closet. These bones belonged to his great-grandson Jude."

From what I could learn of Cousin Jude, he was a bit of a character. As the story goes, Jude was one of the twelve grandsons of one of the most famous and richest men in all the land. (Yep, that was my great uncle Abe.) Jude was a big partier; he liked to take a walk on the wild side every now and again. It was not so much with drugs or booze, but he loved women. Tall, small, young, old ... it didn't seem to matter much to Jude.

§

One day Cousin Jude got tired of the ho hum of the city life, so he called up an old friend named Hal and said, "Let's get away." It would have to be some place remote and discreet since Jude was, by then, governor of the province he lived in. So off they went to some little out-of-the-way town, looking for a good time.

While in that place, Jude met a girl and asked her to be his wife. After a whirlwind romance and a short newly-wed period, she gave birth to three sons. Their first son's name was Ed. Cousin Ed was a bit of a rebel-rouser himself. You know what they say: "The fruit never falls far from the tree." "Like father, like son." What most people don't tend to realize is that for every seed you sow, you're going to get a harvest. So we should all be mindful of the seeds we sow, because one day we'll have to eat the harvest for dinner. Too bad Cousin Ed didn't think that far ahead!

Ed did slow down long enough to get married. They say he married one of the local girls whose name was Tammy Martha Canaan. But other than marrying Tammy, Ed lived life with a reckless abandon … until one day it all caught up with him, and his harvest came in. He suddenly dropped dead.

As I said earlier, the rumor mill had it that God had killed him. This left his young wife behind alone, with no husband and no children. Poor Tammy! Whatever was she going to do? That was where the real-life soap opera part began.

Divinely Dysfunctional

Tammy's father-in-law Jude tried to help out as much as he could. He talked to his other son Owen, Ed's younger brother, about marrying his brother's wife and giving her children, to preserve his brother's name. This was in accordance with the custom and culture of the time. The nearest male relative of the deceased was to impregnate his dead relative's wife, in order to continue his bloodline.

Owen was against this idea from the start. *No way!* he thought to himself. *I want nothing to do with keeping my brother's bloodline going. Besides, tell me who wants to father children that really won't be his?* His focus was on his own life, not someone else's.

Owen was too afraid of his father to tell him this, so he concocted a plan to sleep with Tammy Martha but not impregnate her. He had decided he would rather let his semen fall on the ground than to be used to produce a baby for his brother. And that was exactly what he did. He and Tamar were intimate and, then, right at the point of conception, Owen let his semen spill on the ground. This ensured that there was no way he was going to father a baby by her.

As time passed, Owen became more and more abusive of others ... right up to the day when his harvest came in, and he, too, suddenly keeled over dead, just like his brother Ed before him. If you're counting, for Jude, that was now two sons who had died sudden deaths. He was both hurt and concerned for his family. He particularly didn't want anything to happen to his youngest son, given the mystery surrounding the deaths of his older brothers. Jude didn't know if Tammy might be poisoning his boys, bringing some kind of curse on his family, or just what was going on. If she was causing this, he surely didn't want to upset her by just throwing her out in the street. So, being the smart businessman he was, he cut a deal with his dauther-in-law.

"Tammy," he said, "perhaps you can try again, this time with my youngest son, Shell, once he comes of age [he was still a young boy]. But, for now, why not go back and live with your parents until I call for you."

This didn't leave Tammy much of an alternative, so she gathered her things and agreed to move back into her father's house. Jude, for his part, had done this to buy some time for himself and his family. God only knew if this woman was like a black widow spider that killed its mates.

When a great deal of time passed and nothing was heard from her in-laws, Tammy began to feel as if her father-in-law had tricked her. *He never intended on maintaining my husband's bloodline,* she brooded. She was both hurt and angered by this and didn't know what to do about it. Then one day a friend told her that Jude's wife had died, and he and his buddy Hal were headed out of town for one of their so-called "business trips." Maybe this was her chance to reason with Jude.

But maybe he will just lie to me again, she reasoned, *or try some other trick on me.* So Tammy came up with a trick of her own to play on her ole tricky father-in-law. She decided to go ahead of the two men to the town where they were headed and set a trap for Jude. She would need a disguise so that he wouldn't recognize her, so she covered her hair with a scarf, put on some sexy clothes, took off the wedding band she had faithfully worn until then, and waited for them to come to town. The trap was set.

Tammy was counting on her father-in-law's reputation of being a lady's man. So, dressed like a hooker, she paced up and down the street he would be going by. Sure enough, Jude noticed her and inquired about her services. "How much, young lady?" he asked.

Tammy, the undercover prostitute, replied wisely, "You tell me."

"How about some livestock?" Jude proposed. "It's better than money because it keeps giving a return."

The undercover prostitute agreed, but added, "How do I know you'll pay?"

Jude said, "What do you want to hold for a deposit until I return with the livestock?"

She said, "Give me that fancy cane of yours and that medallion that you have around your neck as a deposit." Jude agreed to her terms, and they were intimate.

Tammy returned to her home, took off her disguise, and went about her life, such as it was. Days later, Jude sent Hal back to the place where he had met the hooker to give her the promised livestock and collect his things, but Hal couldn't find her. While trying to be as discreet as possible, he asked some of the locals where the prostitutes lived who worked the area, and, much to his surprise, he was told that there were no prostitutes in that area. Puzzled, Hal returned home with Jude's livestock.

When Hal told Jude what had happened, he, too, thought it was quite odd. But rather than keep looking for the prostitute and risk his reputation being further tarnished, he decided to call off the search for this mystery woman. He felt it certainly would not be in his best interests for everyone to know that the governor of their province had been scouring the countryside looking for a prostitute. Gee, doesn't that sound like something taken right out of today's headlines!

When several months had passed and there was no news of a mystery girl claiming that she was owed livestock, Jude thought the matter must be over. Then one day he heard a story about a woman who had pretended to be a prostitute just to trick a man into impregnating her. He thought this was an outrage and demanded that the woman be punished for such a terrible deed. Little did he know that the woman in question was his own daughter-in-law and that he was the man she had tricked.

News of this matter had gotten out, evidentially because Tammy's neighbors had been curious about how a widow woman with no prospects for marriage and even no dates could get pregnant. Was she claiming an immaculate conception? Those nosey neighbors dug out the truth of the matter and quickly spread the news.

Jude, not having a clue that the woman everyone was talking about was his daughter-in-law and feeling that he could not sit idly by and allow this injustice to go unpunished, formed a committee to investigate the matter and bring the woman to justice. The committee learned where the woman lived, and they went to her house. They interrogated her, demanding that she tell them who the unknown father of her child was, but she declined to answer them.

Now they threatened her: "If you don't tell us and tell us now, we'll have no other choice but to put you in prison, and you can imagine what might happen to you there."

Finally, Tammy said, "I will give some items that can be used for identification purposes, but you must see to it that the governor himself gets them." The men agreed and took what she gave them straight to Governor Jude.

When the committee returned, Jude asked them what had happened to the woman who perpetrated the crime against the unsuspecting gentleman. They said, "She didn't tell us his name, but she did give us some personal items of his that we can use for identification."

"Good!" Jude said, "Let me see them." When he opened the bag to see what was inside, his jaw nearly dropped to the ground.

"What is it, Governor?" one committee member asked.

He shouted, "Everybody out ... except for Hal!"

After the room had cleared, he gave the bag to Hal and said to him, "Look inside." Hal looked, and his eyes got as big as saucers.

Then Jude said, "Take them out of the bag and let me inspect them." There they were, as big as day, his medallion and his special walking cane. At this point little doubt remained as to who the mystery woman was ... or so they thought.

Jude told Hal to bring the woman to him so that she could face the music. Somehow I don't think he was prepared for the song that was about to be played. When Hal brought Tammy in to see him, Jude was not pleased. He said to her, "What do you want?"

"You sent for me," Tammy said, "and that's why I'm here."

"No!" he shouted. "There is some mistake. I did not send for you. I sent for a prostitute." Tammy just stood there looking at him.

After what seemed like a long time, Tammy opened her mouth and said, "I'm really not a whore. I just didn't want my husband's bloodline to be forgotten."

As if things weren't already shocking enough, now this! Jude thought to himself. After getting over his shock, he said, "Tammy, you were the righteous one, and I was the evil one. I didn't keep my word to you, as I should have, concerning my youngest son, Shell. You had every right to be hurt and angry with me, since all you were trying to do was to keep my dead son's bloodline alive. Please forgive me."

Tammy said, "And please forgive me, Jude, for I should not have deceived you." Jude soon issued Tammy Martha a public pardon, so that all would know he had fully cleared her name.

A few months later, the much-anticipated moment finally arrived, and news spread that Tammy had given birth to healthy twin boys. Everyone was very excited, but even concerning the birthing, there is a story to tell.

As Tammy was giving her next-to-the-last push before delivery, out popped one of the boy's arms. Since everyone knew, by this time, that she was having twins, they had devised a plan to tell which one was delivered first (and would, therefore, be favored). When that arm came out, the midwife reached for some red string, as had been planned, and quickly tied it around that little arm.

Then, even as the midwife announced that the little fellow with the red string was the winner, his arm, just as abruptly as it had appeared, slipped back into the womb. "If there was to be some drama with anybody's baby, it would certainly be Tammy's," the midwife was heard to say.

As the birthing process continued, Tammy delivered one bouncing baby boy, followed by his twin brother. What came as a surprise to everyone was that the baby boy with the red string wrapped around his arm was the second to be delivered, not the first.

Since the first one was so feisty, they named him Perez (which means "ready to break out"). His brother, who was a little more laid back, they called Zaine, which means "colorful or bright." Over time the boys grew into fine young men.

This was especially important since their beginnings had been so shaky, with a mom who pretended to be a whore but wasn't one really, and a father who also doubled as their grandfather. Despite all this, those boys brought honor back to Jude's household, successfully erasing the bad memories of their two deceased older brothers—Ed and Owen.

Perez, just as his name implied, was quite the go-getter and an honorable man, to boot. So I guess it's true what they say: "All is well that ends well."

Through all of this, I was getting some valuable lessons. If those guys could overcome their rocky start, then so could anyone. Most would have easily and quickly labeled them as dysfunctional. The truth is that they were *Divinely Dysfunctional.*

CHAPTER 6

NARCY AND NICE

*Change what you do and you'll
change the result you get.*

rofessor Jones, once again, opens the class. "Well, these lectures have been so interesting and enlightening that we surely don't want to waste any more time. Come, Dr. Divine. Continue with your wonderful theme: 'Good Dysfunction.' "

Thank you. The tussle between those twin boys in the womb of my ancestor Tammy was similar to another story I heard from an early age that related to yet another ancestor and yet another "dysfunctional" relative.

As fate would have it, Jude's father had also been a twin, and he, too, tussled with his brother in their mother's womb. Looks like lightning did strike twice in the same family.

§

Jude's father's name was Yaakov, and his twin brother's name was Harry. Theirs was a complicated story, as most of ours are. The twin's mother was Becky. Let's start with her.

Becky was a very attractive lady from a well-to-do family. For the most part, she had a fairly standard childhood. Not much is known about the inner workings of their family dynamics, other than the fact that she had an older brother named Lanny, whom she was very close to.

From all appearances, Becky seemed happy. Her beauty was what attracted her husband Ike to her, and, after a whirlwind romance, they were married.

Divinely Dysfunctional

Ike was about twenty-five years Becky's senior, but their age difference didn't seem to matter much to them, though some questioned her motives for marrying an older man.

Ike's job required him to travel from time to time, and on one notable occasion Becky traveled with him. She could be a bit bossy and demanding at times, but Ike didn't let it bother him. One evening they were out to dinner with some very important people Ike was hoping to do business with, Ike was asked the question: "Is this your wife?" and he jokingly replied, "No, she's my sister." As you can imagine, the evening went downhill after that.

Ike later assured Becky that it had just been a joke, but she didn't think it was funny. To her, it was offensive and disrespectful, and she had to wonder how he really felt in his heart. It is said that every joke has an ingredient of truth mixed in.

Time passed. Ike and Becky had always talked about having a family one day, and eventually those desires came true. Becky was pregnant, and it was twin boys. However, it was not a pleasant pregnancy. Morning sickness seemed to be the order of the day, and there was lots of kicking and tumbling going on inside her. It almost seemed as if the boys were in a wrestling match, and her stomach was the ring.

The day of delivery was no different. The hospital staff reported that as one twin was on his way out, the other twin pulled him back in and came out before him. Yaakov was believed to have held his brother's heel during birth, so that he could come out first. Myth or mystery ... who knows? But it had definitely seemed like a competition from the day of conception. All we know for sure is that Becky gave birth to two rambunctious boys.

As the boys grew, their personalities began to emerge. Harry was very artful at entrapment, and nothing was safe from his cunningness. The slightly younger Yaakov was extremely charming and yet very deceitful.

Each parent had their favorite. Dad liked the outdoors, as did Harry, so Ike favored his firstborn. Mom chose the would-be underdog, Yaakov, as her project. This fueled competition and brought out Becky's darker side. Perhaps she had never really forgiven Ike for the out-of-town dinner incident. Whatever the case, it was now Game On!

Divinely Dysfunctional

As the boys grew and got older, Yaakov's ego got bigger. His mother told him that since Harry was the elder twin he would be given the family endowment. Becky knew this would fuel a fire inside of her favorite son. "I don't think he deserves it," she said.

"Me either," Yaakov agreed, "but what can be done about it?"

What Becky said next surprised Yaakov. "We can get your father to give you the endowment."

"But, Mother," he said, "you and I both know father would never agree to that."

"Yes, he will," she insisted, "if we have a plan and stick to it."

Yaakov hadn't realized until that moment that his lovely mother wasn't above chicanery to achieve her goals, but he was about to find out just how far she would go.

Ike was getting up in age by this time, and his eyesight was growing quite dim. If he had been diagnosed, I'm sure they would have said that he was "legally blind." This played perfectly into Becky's plan of deception. She was very detailed about her instructions to

Yaakov and demanded that he carry them out with pinpoint precision.

"First," she said, "I'll send Harry off on a hunt to find a prize trophy for his father to relish, something that he would absolutely love to have mounted and hung in the parlor. This will take your brother far away from home, and his hunt will last all day."

Becky paused only for a moment, then continued. "The minute he's gone, I want you to go and get a goat from the neighbors. We will kill it and make your father's favorite dish, curried goat.

"'Next, I want you to cover your entire body with dirt, goat blood and urine. Put it everywhere … in your hair, under your nails and behind your ears."

"Mother," Yaakov protested, "I understand that this will make me smell like my brother, but is it enough? Our body types are different. What happens when father touches me? He'll know."

"Just do as I say, son," Becky insisted, "and let me handle the rest."

While Yaakov was doing as he had been instructed, Becky was busy stitching together animal skins for her son to wear as arm bands. This would disguise his skin in case his father touched him. The plan was set, the meal was prepared, and Yaakov had been given his lines and had dressed in his costume. Now it was ready, set, action!

Ike was in bed resting when a knock came at the door. "Who is it?" he called.

"Father, it's me—Harry," Yaakov lied.

"Come in, son," his father said. And he went in.

"What do you want, my son?" Ike asked.

Yaakov answered on cue, "I've brought you your favorite dish, father, curried goat."

"Oh, everyone knows I love curried goat," Ike said, "Bring it close, son."

As Yaakov approached the bed, Ike reached out to touch his arm and hand. Then he sniffed loudly, taking in a deep breath of the air and with it the smells Yaakov had smeared over himself. "You feel like Harry," his father said, "and you smell like Harry, but you sound like Yaakov."

Standing in the shadows outside the door to the room, Becky breathed a silent prayer. Then she was startled when Ike called for her. "Becky, will you come into my room please!" When there was no response, Ike called again, "Becky, can you come up here!" Still she stood quietly in the shadows, watching the whole production—her production—play out.

"Harry!" Ike said.

"Yes, father, I'm here," Yaakov answered. "I've brought you this meal before leaving. I'm ready to leave home and set out to find my own path in life."

This thought was a heavy one for Ike. "Are you sure, son?" he asked.

"Yes, father, I am," Yaakov said.

"Well, it seems that you've made your mind up. As the eldest, you are due to receive the family endowment. Take it, son, and use it wisely. You have my blessings."

It was over ... or was it? For the moment, it seemed that Yaakov (with the help of his mother) had successfully deceived his father, stolen the family endowment and robbed his brother of his rightful inheritance. As can be imagined, however, when Harry found out what they had done, he was furious and vowed to kill his brother the moment he saw him.

Becky could never allow this to happen, so she immediately sent Yaakov away to live with her brother Lanny and his family. Yaakov was well received by his Uncle Lanny's family, especially his two daughters. (No, they were not twins, in case you were wondering). Yaakov was smitten by the younger sister, Racine. He thought she was an angel. Her older sister, Lee, was far less desirable to him.

Yaakov worked as a ranch hand for his Uncle Lanny, just so he could be close to Racine. His uncle was glad to get the free help. Lanny knew he had eyes for Racine and decided to use that fact to his advantage.

For his part, Yaakov worked diligently with the intent of eventually asking for Racine's hand in marriage. Yes, he was going to ask his uncle if he could marry his daughter (his first cousin). Her aunt would then become her mother-in-law, and his Uncle Lanny would become his father-in-law. Wow! Talk about a mixed-up family!

Yaakov told another ranch hand of his devious plan to have Racine as his wife, and the man said he knew that Racine's bedroom was upstairs, the second door on the left. Yaakov said he was going to sneak into that room and sleep with her. When Lanny learned that Racine was no longer a virgin, to save face and embarrassment, he would agree to their marriage. What Yaakov didn't know was that Lanny overhead this plan and that night had Racine and Lee switch rooms.

In the middle of the night Yaakov crept into the bedroom he thought was Racine's and slept with the woman in that bed. The next day Lanny called Yaakov into the house. "Yaakov," he said, "my daughter is no longer a virgin because you slept with her."

"That's true, uncle," Yaakov admitted, "I did."

"Now," Lanny continued, "to make her an honorable woman, you must marry her."

"I am certainly willing to do that," Yaakov said, trying not to look too happy about the matter. The truth was that he could hardly contain himself.

"Daughters, come down here," Lanny called. "One of you has a new brother-in-law, and the other has a new husband." His words seemed to hang in the air, and Yaakov wished he would get to the punch line.

"Racine," Lanny said, turning to his younger daughter, "congratulate your sister Lee on her engagement to be married to Yaakov."

Yaakov couldn't believe what he was hearing. "No!" he protested. "Wait! This is a mistake! I slept with Racine not Lee."

Lanny was not shaken by this protestation, "Well, son," he continued, "didn't you get in the bed upstairs, the second door on the left?"

"Yes, uncle, I did," Yaakov said, hoping this would settle the matter.

"Then you're right, Yaakov," Uncle Lanny said, " a mistake was made, and you made it. When you planned to trick me into allowing you to marry Racine, I had the two girls change rooms. So it was you who got tricked and not me. Now you have no choice in the matter. You must marry Lee. And that is final!"

Sadly and painfully, Yaakov began to realize that his mother and uncle were both masters of trickery.

Having no other recourse, Yaakov went forward with his marriage to Lee. To top matters off, as a result of his one-night stand with her, Lee was pregnant. Yaakov wasn't mean to Lee, but he wasn't very kind to her either. Under these conditions, nine months seemed like forever, but eventually Lee gave Yaakov his firstborn son.

Yaakov was delighted to have a son, but he still wanted Racine. Since the day of his betrothal, he had been planning his divorce from Lee and his marriage to Racine. In between those two events, Yaakov fathered several children, some by Lee and others not. D-Day did eventually come, and he divorced Lee and married his sister-in-law and first cousin Racine. Now, that was a close-knit family!

As Yaakov's children grew, he spent more quality time with them, especially the older boys. He wanted to prepare them for life. His oldest son, Rube, always had lots of questions. One day he asked, "Father, when are we going to see our grandparents, your parents?"

"I'm not sure, son," Yaakov answered.

"Why has it been so long since you've spoken with them or Uncle Harry?" Rube queried.

"It's complicated, son," was his father's reply.

Divinely Dysfunctional

"Father," Rube insisted, "you're always saying how important family is. Doesn't that mean yours too?"

The words went through Yaakov's heart like an ice pick, and he answered truthfully for the first time, "Yes, son, family is very important, but I did a terrible thing to my family."

"Father," Rube continued, "you have taught us that mistakes happen, even when you're trying your best, and that when you make a mistake, you just have to own up to it, learn from it and move on."

"Yes, son. You're right. I said that," Yaakov admitted.

"Then, Father, don't you think your family will forgive you?" Rube asked.

"I don't know, son," Yaakov said, shaking his head in dismay. "I just don't know."

"It's a lot to forgive," Yaakov continued.

"Well, how will you know whether or not they will forgive you if you never ask for forgiveness?" Rube was continuing with his questioning, but Yaakov didn't mind. He loved Rube's inquisitiveness, and the boy was right about this.

"You're right, Rube," he admitted, "I'll ask," and that night he told the rest of the family to be ready to leave in the morning because he was taking them back to where he came from.

True to his word, the next morning Yaakov and his family set out on the long trip back to his parents' house. While they were traveling, Racine had time to ask, "What do you hope to accomplish?"

"Well," Yaakov said, "first of all, I need to make things right. I need to repent to my father, mother and brother ... if ... if they'll hear me."

"Are you serious about being sorry for what you did?" she asked.

"Yes, certainly!" he replied.

"Then they'll hear your sincere heart," she assured him.

Their conversation was interrupted at this point because the company seemed to have stopped moving. "What's the problem, dear?" Racine asked.

"I have no idea," he said. "I'll go see what I can find out."

While Yaakov was out surveying the issue, a stranger came by. "Is everything all right?" he asked.

Divinely Dysfunctional

"I don't know," Yaakov answered him.

"Where are you going?" inquired the stranger.

"My family and I are traveling to my parents' house," Yaakov explained. "I have very important business there, and I haven't been there in years."

"I'll tell you what," the stranger said, "about a mile in the direction you're traveling there's a farmhouse with a vehicle. You could steal it and be on your way in no time."

"No way!" Yaakov said.

"Okay," the man said, "what if I steal it and give it to you?"

"No!" Yaakov said, wrestling with his own conscious about whether he should accept this strange offer or not.

"Okay, what if … ," the stranger began another question, but Yaakov cut him off before he could finish.

"That's enough!" Yaakov said sternly. "Please leave us alone now!" And, with that, the mysterious stranger left as quickly as he had come.

Troubled by all of this, Rube asked, "Father, why wouldn't you let that man help you?"

"Actually, son," Yaakov answered, "that might have been a test."

"A test, father?"

"Yes, son, a test, a test to see if I've really changed. I know now that I have to change what I do in order to change what I get."

Yaakov and his family continued on their trip. When they arrived at his parents' house, he was first met by his brother. Yes, Harry, the one who had vowed to kill him on sight. Now, instead of doing him harm, Harry reached out and embraced his brother and told him just how much he had missed him. Yaakov repented, and Harry forgave him, as did his parents.

Harry told Yaakov, "It took tremendous courage for you to do what you did, and God will reward you."

"He already has," Yaakov said.

I have held that story very tight in my heart ever since I heard it. We all have our own story to tell. Someone may have called you or, at least considered you to be, dysfunctional. The truth is that you are *Divinely Dysfunctional.*

CHAPTER 7

FAVORSCHISM

That sounds like a YOU problem.

*P*rofessor Jones asked, "Are you ready for another of these fascinating lectures?" When there was a cheer from the student body, he proceeded. "Then, let's welcome Dr. Divine and his subject: 'Good Dysfunction.' "

Some things aren't hereditary, but they are generational. Yaakov had his own issues compounded by those of his family, but what about the individual who has no overt issues of their own, but their family does? Some might be wondering. That was the case with one of Yaakov's sons named Jay.

§

Jay was Yaakov's favorite son, a son whom he adored. Just as with any other family, when one child is exalted above the others, tensions arise and animosity thrives. It was well known that Racine was the apple of Yaakov's eye, so it should have come as no great surprise when the children she bore him were favored as well. She gave him two boys: Benny, the youngest of all his children, and Jay, who was next to the youngest.

Benny often received a pass from his other brothers simply because he was the baby of the family. Jay, on the other hand, received a double portion of jealousy. As a boy, he had big dreams of doing big things, and his brothers didn't seem to aspire to the heights that he hoped for his own life. These factors, along with the normal sibling rivalry, created a recipe for danger.

Divinely Dysfunctional

As with many families, hand-me-down clothes from one generation to the next were commonplace with Yaakov and his large clan. But Yaakov broke that time-honored tradition for Jay, giving him a very special garment, and this caused a terrible uproar.

The cold of the winters was harsh on the adults, but even more so on the children, and that winter was no exception. Jay had been experiencing a few health issues, but really not much more than the others before him. Whatever the rational, Yaakov decided to buy Jay a hand-made sweater, to help him through the season. No one else had ever received such preferential treatment. There were ten older brothers, and not one of them had ever received anything like it.

Parents must be mindful of the atmosphere they are creating in their homes and in the individual lives of their family members. We must try to give thought to the whole situation rather than focusing on one particular circumstance. Okay, now, back to Jay.

When Jay received that new sweater, everyone was instantly upset with him, when perhaps they should have been upset with Yaakov instead. To them, it seemed obvious that Jay had done something to present himself as being better and more worthy than the rest of them or he would not have received such special recognition. In fact, that was not the case. Unfortunately, sometimes a person who is favored gets blamed for being favored, simply because the fact of their favor cannot be explained or understood. *Why them and not me?* This single event was enough to draw the ire of the whole family to Jay.

But there was more. Not only did Jay have ideals, but he also had dreams to corroborate what he believed. One night he had a dream that he was going to become a high-ranking official. He would have tremendous power and authority. He would become a great success. If the story had stopped there, it wouldn't have been so bad, but in his dream, his brothers had bowed down and worshipped him. They weren't just proud of him. They didn't just boast to others that they were his family. That was still not enough. They had to worship at his feet. Wow! Talk about crazy dreams!

Now things quickly got worse. Jay, inspired by his dream, actually gathered his brothers together and told them about it. When he had finished, Rube, the oldest, said, "Let me make sure I understand this correctly. We're going to be your servants?"

"No!" Jay said. "We're family. I would never allow that. You're just going to worship me because I am the greatest thing to ever happen to our family."

"Oh, is that all?" Rube replied smugly, and the other brothers were so angry they could not even speak. Now they hated Jay all the more.

Jay then had yet another dream. In this one, even his parents bowed to him, and he told the entire family about it. His brothers could not wait to hear their father's response. Yaakov sat quietly until Jay had finished, and then he said only one perplexed word, "Interesting!" And, with that, he got up and walked out of the room, dismayed and confused.

"Interesting?" one of the brothers said. "That's it? It was just 'interesting?' " They were totally disgusted with the boy. It was from that moment that Jay's brothers decided that he had to go. They didn't discuss among themselves how they would do it, but they knew it had to be done.

Months passed by with no major interruptions. Then spring had come again. The flowers were blooming, and the bees were buzzing. Everything in nature was busy, and so, too, were Jay's brothers. They were busy planning his disappearance.

One of the brothers said, "We should drop him down one of those dry wells on the property. We wouldn't kill him, just leave him there for a while. Maybe that will straighten him out." They all agreed. Now all they needed to decide was when.

One day the brothers were out in the fields working. It was very hot that day, and Racine asked Jay to take some water to his brothers. He gathered up as much water as he could carry, and out he went. Rube and the others saw Jay coming from far away and decided that this was the perfect time to put their evil plan into action.

As soon as Jay got close enough, the brothers jumped him and bound him hand and foot. They also put tape over his mouth so that he couldn't be heard crying out for help.

Amazingly, despite the hot temperature that day, Jay was wearing his prize sweater. They snatched it off of him and then took him, as planned, to a dry well on the back of the property. Once they reached the well, they told him that if he ever told anyone what they had done, they would kill him. Then they lowered him down into that dry well.

The brothers then tore the sweater and rubbed blood on it. They would tell their father that an animal must have attacked his beloved son.

When they got home, they told this concocted tale, but they never in their wildest dreams could have imagined how grief-stricken their father would be over the loss of Jay. Racine was crying, but Yaakov was totally overwhelmed. All through the night he could be heard lamenting and crying out to God.

The next morning Rube headed out early with the other brothers to see if Jay had made it through the night and, if so, how. As they got close to the well they could hear their brother crying out to God for help. Rube was convicted in his heart for what he and his brothers had done and quickly got Jay out of the well.

Then, as Rube was trying to figure out their next move, he heard a great disturbance on the road that ran next to their property. They all moved closer to investigate. It was a traveling carnival that just happened to be passing through at that moment.

Rube suggested that Jay go with the carnival and warned his young brother that this was his only chance for survival. He reminded him that the others said they would kill him if he returned. So off Jay went as a carnival hand or "carny," as they are called in the business.

Time passed quickly as the carnival traveled from town to town. Jay became a vital part of the set-up and break-down everywhere they went. In the process, he grew from a frail four-teen-year-old frightened boy into a well-built knowledgeable young man in his early twenties.

Then, one day, in one of the towns where they performed, a man noticed how hard-working Jay was. "Hello, son," he said. "My name is Judge Potts."

"Hello, sir," Jay politely answered.

"I've been watching how diligent you are," the judge told him, "and I want to offer you a job."

"Doing what, sir?" Jay asked.

"As a page in my courtroom,' the judge said. "We could use a diligent young man such as yourself, and, if you want, you could live with my wife and me in our home." It was the best offer Jay had received in years, so he gladly accepted.

Working as a page was much less strenuous than carny work, and Jay learned a lot more too. Judge Potts noticed that Jay seemed quite comfortable in a courtroom setting, so he entered him into an apprentice program. Jay was ecstatic with the opportunity of learning more about the law and, quite possibly, even becoming a judge himself one day.

Everything was going along great … until one night when Jay came home late. The judge wasn't home either, but Mrs. Potts was. She, too, had taken notice of Jay's growth, and suddenly Jay found himself once again in a situation where someone else was trying to do as they wished with him.

But Jay was determined not to be a victim this time. He ran so fast out of that house that he caught the shirt he was wearing on something, and it tore. This left Mrs. Potts as a woman scorned, and they say that "Hell hath no fury like Mrs. Potts."

When the judge got home that night, his wife told him that Jay had attacked her. When she screamed for help, she said, he ran and tore his shirt in the process. Honestly, the judge didn't know what to make of this accusation. He kicked Jay out of their home, but he didn't press charges against him. In this way, Jay was able to finish his apprenticeship and receive his law degree.

Later, Judge Potts gave Jay a favorable reference for a seat on the appellant court bench, and he was accepted. Wow! Jay had achieved his dream of being a high-ranking official, and this made him reflect on his family, especially his little brother Benny. He missed his family ... all of them.

Years passed with Jay sitting on the Court of Appeals bench, hearing cases, argument after argument. Some were easy to settle, and others were not. Then one day a land dispute was placed on the calendar for trial. It involved neighbors disputing over who owned a well that had been dry for fifteen years or so but was now flowing like an underground stream. *A once-dry well that is now prosperous and flowing ... that's me,* Jay thought to himself. This also caused Jay to remember his time in the dry well.

When the plaintiffs were called forward, Jay couldn't believe his eyes. It was Rube and three of his brothers. So much time had passed that they didn't recognize him, but he was positive they were, in fact, his brothers.

Jay spoke first. "This is a case between land-owners." Turning to Rube, he asked, "Are you one of the landowners?"

"No," Rube said, "my father is, but he is old and unable to attend the court session."

"I will not hear this case without the landowners in question being present," Jay insisted.

To this, Rube protested so vigorously that the judge ordered him to be held in contempt and sentenced him to spend thirty days in jail. In his mind, it was not a matter of vengeance, but rather of order.

The other brothers were ordered to go home and get their father and the rest of his family and return with them to the courtroom so that their case could be properly tried. When the brothers got home, they told their father all that had happened. Yaakov said, "I've lost one son, I'll not lose another." So he and his sons headed back to go before the judge.

When their time came to appear, the bailiff was instructed to ask if the entire family was present. Yaakov said, "No, it's just myself and three sons."

"Aren't there more of you?" the bailiff asked.

"Yes," Yaakov answered, "I have twelve … make that eleven sons in all. One is here in jail, and three are with me now."

"But the judge said that you are to appear with *all* your sons," said the bailiff. "Now go, and don't come back without the others."

Yaakov thought this request odd, but he didn't want any more problems, so he headed back home.

Once Yaakov arrived home, Racine wanted further explanation about all that was going on and why. Yaakov shared with her that, despite the odd request, he was going to comply. Racine said, "But why must you take my baby? I've already lost one son."

Meanwhile, Jay was wondering how he would handle seeing his father after so many years. What would be his father's reaction? Would the shock kill him? Would he want to kill the other brothers for what they had done to him? These and other questions whirled in his mind. One thing he knew for certain: it would be great to see Benny again.

At the same time, Yaakov was reassuring Racine that he would return home shortly with their baby boy safe and sound. "You promise?" she asked.

"I promise, dear," he assured her, and with that, he headed out with his sons on their trip back to the courthouse.

Back again in the courtroom, their case was called. Turning to Yaakov, the judge asked, "'Are you the landowner, sir?"

"Yes, your honor, I am," Yaakov said.

"Are these all your sons?" Jay asked next.

"All except two," Yaakov responded.

"And where are those two?" Jay demanded.

Yaakov said, "You have one here in the jail, and the other ... the other ... my other son is dead." Yaakov wept as he spoke these words, and Jay turned his head and wiped tears from his own eyes.

The judge motioned to the bailiff to bring Rube in, and Yaakov and his other sons embraced him. Then the judge said, "Before I rule on the matter of the property, there is something that I must do. I need to speak with your youngest son alone in my chambers. Which one is he?"

Alarmed, Yaakov said, "Please, sir, I beg of you: don't take my son. Please!" He fell to the floor and bowed before the judge.

Upon seeing their father's example, the other brothers did likewise. Bowing in unison, they said, "Please, your honor, be gracious to our family!"

The judge said, "Bailiff, please escort the young man into my chambers." Then, to Yaakov and his other sons, he said, "I will return shortly."

When Jay entered his chambers, Benny was standing near his desk. Jay said, "So, you're Benny?"

"How did you know my name?" Benny asked.

Ignoring this question, Jay continued with his purpose, "Benny, you were but a baby when your brother Jay left."

Divinely Dysfunctional

"You mean ... *was killed*, don't you?" Benny said.

"No," Jay answered, "I mean *left*."

After a short pause, he continued, "Your brother left the house that day to take your other brothers something to drink because it was so hot and they were working hard in the fields."

"That's the same thing Father and Mother told me as I grew older," Benny said, "but how do you know this, judge?"

Trembling with emotion, the man in robes said, "I know this, Benny, because I am your brother. I am Jay."

As this was still sinking in, he added, "You have a long scar under your chin because when you were a baby you ran and fell."

Astonished, Benny replied, "Jay, how can it be you? Papa said you were killed by wild animals."

"I was not killed, brother," Jay answered. "I'm very much alive. And I have missed you greatly, baby brother." The two men fell into each other's arms and wept.

A little later, Jay walked out into the court-room holding Benny's hand. They walked right up to Yaakov, and Jay said to him, "Father, you once again have all of your twelve sons with you. It is I, Jay, and God has brought me back to you." With that, Yaakov and his twelve sons embraced each other and wept together.

Thomas Jefferson once said, "The dreams of the future are better than the history of the past." Jay's life was the embodiment of these words. There can be no doubt that many would have called his family dysfunctional. The truth is that they were *Divinely Dysfunctional.*"

CHAPTER 8

RUMOR SCARS

Your mishap could be your miracle in the making.

gain Professor Jones begins the class. "Wow! I trust that you have been enjoying these lectures as much as I have. They are enlightening, entertaining and informative ... all at the same time. This man has wisdom, and we would all benefit from it. Dr. Divine, thank you for these truths, and now we give you the platform for another exciting round." The students applaud as Dr. Divine takes the podium.

Thank you. Early on in this series I told you about the circumstances of my birth. I was born to a teenage mother, and my real father was unknown. I have had to hear my whole life what everyone else thought of my mother, whose name is May, and yet no one has truly known her story. What was her side of this supposedly-tall tale? And what effect did this whole episode have on her?

Picture, if you can, a small-town girl who had only recently become a teenager. Her family was rather well-to-do by the standards of the day, although they did not live exorbitant lives in any sense of the word. They were a good, wholesome family that was known in their community due to their work in ministry. You see, Joel, Mom's father and my grandfather, was a preacher, as was his brother and their father before them. In fact, he came from a long line of preachers.

As for Mom's mother (my grandmother), Amy, she, too, had a heart for ministry. One might be able to imagine that this family was constantly involved in something at the church or something to do with the church. Ministry became a part of the life of each member of the household.

Divinely Dysfunctional

Other than this fact, Mom had a fairly normal childhood. She learned to cook, clean and tend to the home, like other young women. She had always been very strong-willed, some might even say rebellious. As the days came and went, she noticed that there were changes in her body. She was becoming a woman.

According to the customs of the day in her homeland, when a girl had her first period she was considered to be a woman and was, therefore, ready to be engaged to be married. The thinking behind this was that a couple that was married at an early age would have a long and happy life together, while also removing the temptation of them just having casual sex with someone for its own sake. To some, this might sound pretty restrictive, but it was quite the norm for her culture.

So here Mom was, about the age of a girl in junior high school, ready to begin her life as a newlywed. One of the locals named Joe was interested in her, and he appeared to be a nice, hard-working carpenter. Although he was about ten years her senior, after a period of being checked out by the family, he was allowed to ask for Mom's hand in marriage, and everyone agreed. It was to be. There was a wedding to be planned.

Everything seemed to be set. Mom's parents had not only given their consent; they may have actually set the date. Parents had such rights in those days. Anyway, all appeared to be going according to schedule.

Then one day, while Mom was daydreaming about her upcoming wedding, as do all young girls, something happened. She was picturing who would be in attendance, what they would be wearing, if the weather would cooperate, what she hoped for in the food, the flowers, and, of course, the dress. Then suddenly a vision of a very different dress than the one she had always dreamed of appeared before her. This dress seemed bigger than the one she had always pictured. Of course the dress was still white, but it seemed wider in the waist area. In fact, it looked a lot like a maternity dress.

As Mom squinted to see better and pondered to understand this strange phenomenon, she fell into a deep trance. While she was in the trance, a stranger appeared to her. He said his name was Gabby and that he had come to give her some news about her future life. Understandably, Mom was a bit apprehensive because she didn't know this man or how he could possibly know anything about her. A thousand different thoughts ran through her mind.

The stranger saw the confused and somewhat fearful look on Mom's face and said to her, "Don't be fearful, May. You have been chosen for a very special assignment." He went on, "I want to explain further to you the vision you just saw of your wedding dress."

How did he know about the vision I saw? Mom thought to herself. He certainly had her attention now.

The stranger went on to tell Mom that she was going to have a baby boy. He said the child would be strong, healthy, wise and famous, and that he would be a king whose rule would extend far past the boundaries of their local area. Mom thought this news was so wonderful that she told the stranger she could hardly wait to share it with her husband-to-be Joe. But to this the stranger replied, "Wait, May, there's more to tell. Joe will not father this baby. This birth will be an unexplainable miracle."

As Mom tried to absorb what she had already heard, the stranger continued, "Your older cousin, Eliza, is six months pregnant with a boy too. You should go and see her."

Mom told the stranger that she would do whatever needed to be done, and once she had spoken those words she awakened. Well, you know how, when you first wake up from a dream, you're still a bit groggy? Surprisingly, Mom was quite clear headed and was feeling something akin to relief. Rather than tell anyone about her recent dream, she thought perhaps she should go and visit her cousin Eliza, as instructed. So she left immediately, without even telling anyone where she was going.

When Mom arrived at her cousin's house, Zack, Eliza's husband, answered the door. Zack told Mom that her cousin had some unbelievable news to share with her. About that time Eliza entered the room with what appeared to be a basketball in her stomach. "Surprise!" she said. "Guess who's going to have a baby?"

As Mom reached out to hug Eliza, she felt a strong kick from her baby. "That's odd," Eliza said. "It felt like the baby jumped with excitement when you got close to me."

Divinely Dysfunctional

When the excitement of the moment had subsided, Eliza continued, "You seem different, May. What's going on with you? I feel like you have some news of your own to share with me. I had a dream that you were pregnant."

With this, Mom fell to her knees and began weeping. "I, too, had a dream that I was pregnant," she said and began telling Eliza all that had happened to her and about the things the stranger had told her. She readily admitted that she didn't fully understand it all or what she should do about it. Eliza just listened intently as Mom went on and on about what this event meant and what it would do to their family.

After hours of talking, Mom told Eliza that she would like to stay and help out around the house until their baby was born. She sent word back home to Joe and her family that she was going to help Eliza with the baby. Those few months flew by, and before they knew it, Eliza had delivered a healthy baby boy, just as had been foretold in her dream. Many family members came to share in this happy occasion.

When the baby was born, everyone just assumed that his name would be Zack, Jr. after his father, but apparently the parents were not in sync. Zack felt so strongly about his position that he hadn't spoken for months about it. Eliza said, "Our son will be named what I heard in a dream to name him, and that was John." Zack finally agreed, and so it was. They had a son named John.

By this time Mom was beginning to show a bit of her own little surprise package, so she thought it best to head back home. Upon arriving there, she first wanted to let her family know about her visitation and the blessing to soon be revealed. Quite naturally, there was some scepticism over her insistence of having no sexual activity, yet somehow being several months pregnant. This issue was far too big to be resolved in one conversation, so she left her parents' home and went to find Joe to speak with him.

Mom soon found Joe, and they began to talk about these recent developments. By the time she had brought him up to speed, he just sat there speechless. "Say something, Joe," she said.

"What do you want me to say?" he replied. "I certainly can't say that I understand what or how or why this happened to us. I've never heard of such a thing in my life, nor do I know of anyone else who's ever heard of such a thing ever taking place. So, what do you want me to say, May? Truthfully, I'm finding this whole thing pretty unbelievable."

Joe paused for a moment, thinking how best to word what he had to say next. There didn't seem to be any good way to say it, so he just blurted it out. "I'm sorry, but there's no way I can marry you under these circumstances. I think it's probably best to just call the wedding off." In order to soften the blow, Joe added, "Don't worry. I won't make a spectacle of you or anything like that. I wouldn't do that to you or to your family. We can just tell everyone that I called the wedding off because I wasn't ready. What I need right now, May, is some time alone, time to process everything you've just told me." And with that, Joe walked away, to be by himself.

Mom was not completely caught off guard by Joe's reaction. She had known that this would be hard for him too, but she had been hoping and praying that perhaps he had received the same epiphany that she and Eliza had. This prayer was soon to be answered.

Days passed with Joe not speaking to Mom regarding any firm decision. Then one night, while tossing and turning in his bed, he began to dream. In his dream, he heard a voice call his name and mention that he was a descendant of royalty. The voice told him not to be afraid to wed Mom, because what she told him was the truth. The baby in her womb was, in fact, a miracle. They were to raise this child together, knowing that he was a miracle and that he was going to help many people.

As soon as he could after he awoke, Joe went to tell Mom his dream. They could marry after all. God had a plan for it. Still uncertain as to how things would ultimately unfold, he and Mom forged ahead with their plans.

In the midst of the re-planning of the wedding, a law was passed that every citizen was to return to the city of his family's origin. This meant that Joe would have to travel back to his hometown just to file his taxes. *What seems like it is going to be a real pain might turn out to be a blessing,* he thought to himself. This would be an opportunity for he and May to get away from all the questions surrounding her pregnancy. So, off they went, Joe and his very pregnant fiancé.

For the most part, it was a fairly uneventful trip. The real adventure didn't begin until they arrived in their destination and tried to find a place to spend the night. That's when all the drama started. No one had so much as a closet that had not already been rented for the night. Finally they found an old smelly barn, but it was better than nothing.

Whether it was the trip, the stress of trying to find housing for the night, the smelly barn or some combination of all of it, something had induced Mom's labor. There they were, in the middle of a big, old drafty barn with no doctors or midwives present, and this much-anticipated visitor was about to arrive at any moment. The thickness of the tense air was only cut by the sound of a newborn baby taking his first breath of air. Actually it was more like a shrill scream, but he had to breathe to do it. Either way, both parents were delighted that the blessed moment had finally come.

There their child was, wrapped in a cloth they had found while sharing his birthing room with barn animals, yet he was the most beautiful sight either of them had ever seen, they later told me. For a few moments, everything seemed rather normal. You had a new father, a new mother and a new bundle of joy. Normal ... that is until some farmers showed up saying they had seen a vision that they would be able to find the next king in that very barn. When they saw me, for some reason they bowed as you would before royalty.

Also, there was an elderly man named Simon who wanted to see this miracle child. He, too, had seen a vision of a new king being born that night. When he saw me, he uttered a prayer of thanksgiving to God for allowing him to see the next world ruler.

Additionally, there was one Ms. Anna, who said that she believed I had been sent to overthrow the existing crooked government. "He is going to be a king like none other!" she shouted. As the questions began all over again about me and the pregnancy, many of Joe's anxieties returned. He needn't have worried. Technically, they were covered because a betrothal was as good as a marriage in that part of the world. And he and Mom did eventually get married and went on to raise a family together.

It couldn't have been easy for either of them, wanting to share with everyone their fantastic story, only to have people jeer and mock at them when they tried. And Mom's sexuality was always a hot topic among the hearsay gang. Who was my real father? Had Mom been unfaithful to Joe? Was she or wasn't she delusional? After all, she was on a very short list of women who claimed they had gotten pregnant without having sex with a man.

But Mom never displayed any anger over these ruthless comments or showed any ill feelings toward the people who offered them. She just quietly smiled and said, "God will handle it." This would-be-promiscuous-sexless-teenage wonder showed quite a bit of character by not reacting to those hurtful words. Perhaps Mom didn't want to be one of the many who continue in the cycle in which hurting people hurt other people. To most everyone, she was a totally dysfunctional mother. The truth is that she was *Divinely Dysfunctional*.

CHAPTER 9

SCHIZOFRIENDLY

I'm not you, nor was I meant to be.

Professor Jones begins, "Dr. Divine, I have to hand it to you. I don't know many people who would be willing to divulge details of their personal life as you have, and all in an effort to help the rest of us realize that there is a little dysfunction in us all. Thank you for that. And please continue."

Good morning. It may surprise you to learn that I have not had many people I would call "very close friends." I have had one very special lady friend whom I have often confided in. Her name is Maggie, and I really like her. Maggie is just a very nice person, and we have always seemed to hit it off. One of the things Maggie and I have in common is our interesting origins. Let me tell you about how we met and how she came to be such a big part of my life.

I was out one day with some associates doing some community work, as I have often done. We were at a clinic, delivering medical supplies and food to those who had come for help. From time to time, I would sit down with some of the patrons and talk with them for hours on end. As I noted earlier, I love people, and I love to hear their stories. So there I was, just sitting and talking with everyone as if we had known each other all our lives.

I always did my best to make everyone I talked with feel better, even to feel as though they were talking to a very old and dear friend, even someone closer than a friend or brother. I wanted to be special to everyone I met. As a result, when people knew we were coming to their community, they would turn out by the droves, just to sit and talk with us for awhile. But the time always seemed to pass so quickly, and before you knew it, I and my friends had to leave.

As we were leaving one of these assignments one day, someone told me about a very remote community that could really use our help. They said there were a lot of troubled people there, people who needed special attention. I was moved by that and agreed that on our next outing we would go to that little remote town to see if we could help.

True to our word, I and my colleagues traveled north to a little town about two hours from our home. When we got to the community, we were greeted by some peddlers begging for money. I, being the generous guy that I am, shared all that I had with me at the time. Then, as was our standard, we also sat and spoke with them about how they got in their situation. I always tried to offer up meaningful words of encouragement and practical advice that the people could apply to their daily lives to keep them from entering a reoccurring cycle.

Among the people there that particular day was a man who had been crippled from birth. My heart really went out to this man, and I said to him, "Sir, what's wrong?"

The man began to explain how he had come to be crippled and that he received little help from others in getting around. Everyone stood very still and watched to see how I would respond to this man.

I listened intently to what he was saying and then responded, "Sir, let me ask you a question: do you want to live the rest of your life as an invalid or as a whole person?"

The man looked quite puzzled by this but finally said, "Why, as a whole person, of course."

"Then quit operating out of a crippled mindset," I said to him. "Get up and get moving, and as you do, others won't mind helping you."

I seemed to have a knack for knowing when all that someone needed was some tough love as opposed to when they needed heartfelt medical care. There were so many there who needed so much.

Normally, in a crowd like that, you would see mostly men, but this town had its fair share of women with problems as well. There were three women who seemed to know each other. I quickly came to refer to them affectionately as "the Three Musketeers." At first glance, you could immediately tell that each of them had experienced a pretty rough go of things in life.

The name of the quiet one was Susan. Susan never really spoke a whole lot to anyone and seemed to be a bit of a loner, except for her relationship with the other two women. She looked as if she hadn't had a good meal in days, so I went over to offer her some food. It was hard to hear her feeble answer as she thanked me for this kindness.

"When was the last time you had a good cooked meal?" I asked.

Susan answered, "I can't remember."

"Well, we will certainly have to change that," I told her.

As Susan ate, we sat and talked.

"May I call you Suzy?" I asked.

"Sure," she said.

"So, Suzy," I continued, "what can I do to help make your life just a little bit better?"

"Better?" she said, "I'd settle for just having a life."

When I asked her what she meant by that, Suzy began to tell me about how she had no hope for the future because of having to live with a life-threatening illness. She told me the story of how she had seen several physicians, and they had all told her the same thing, that her disease was incurable. She told me she was basically living from day to day, waiting to die.

When Suzy had finished, I turned and motioned for Matt, one of my associates, to hand me his bag. When I reached inside the bag and pulled out some samples of a new medicine that had recently been made available and gave them to Suzy, she was so overjoyed that tears ran down her face.

While Suzy and I were talking, her two friends just stood back and observed, but once I had given her the medicine, they ran over to see what it was that had made her so happy. Then Musketeer number two opened her mouth to speak.

"Hey," she said, "my name is Joanna." After a short pause, she continued, "And this is my friend Maggie. I see you've already met Suzy.

Divinely Dysfunctional

That was real nice of you to give her that medicine. What does she owe you?"

"Owe me?" I asked, "why nothing at all."

"You mean you just gave that to her, and you don't want anything in return?" she asked.

"Well," I said, "I do want one thing."

At that point, Maggie interrupted, "Didn't I tell you, Jo? I knew he wanted something for all this. He and his friends weren't doing this for free. That's why they approached Suzy instead of me or you. They thought she was an easy mark."

"Please!" I said, "let me finish."

I paused to get their attention again, and then I continued, "All I want is for Suzy to begin to feel better."

"Are you sure that's all you want?" Maggie said.

"Well, no," I admitted, "I'd like to help the two of you also ... if I can."

I didn't know it at the time, but, according to others in the community, these three women had a pretty sordid past. Many believed that their former profession had been prostitution, and that this was how they happened to know each other in the first place. But a person's past never seemed to matter much to me. I believe that everyone deserves a chance in life, no matter what has happened in their past. And these three ladies were no different.

"So, Joanna," I said, "how did you ladies come to know one another?"

Joanna answered, "Maggie and I have known each other the longest, and then we met Suzy. It was like I had found sisters I never knew I had. Each of us had a pretty rough road alone, so it was good to have the company. God knows my life certainly hasn't been a bowl of cherries. I, too, have been in and out of hospitals, and I still don't know what's wrong with me for sure."

I gave Joanna time to say what was on her heart and then I suggested, "Let Jon here examine you. He's a very qualified member of our team. I'm sure he'll be able to help you."

Once Joanna was being attended to, I next turned my attention toward Maggie and said, "Why don't you tell me about yourself?"

She smiled, but I could sense the tension in her reply. "Well, not much to tell really. I grew up in a town a few miles from here. It's just a small fishing community ... because it's right on the water. There are always plenty of folks coming and going. Nobody really stayed around long, including my father. He walked out on my mom and me when I was pretty young. With no man in the house, we had it rough. My mother did the best she could taking care of us, but when something like that happens, you have to grow up quick. You see and learn things that a child really shouldn't know about until later in life."

Maggie continued, but her words now delved deeper and revealed more personal details. "I have a few demons of my own to deal with. I was an addict, so I've had to steal, lie, trick, manipulate and some other things that I'd rather not mention, just to survive. That's why I'm not too quick to trust other people. It seems like everybody's got an angle."

"Is that what you thought I was doing, working an angle?" I asked her.

"Yep," she admitted, "everybody wants someone to give them something."

"What do *you* want to be given, Maggie?" I asked.

"Me?" she said, "I don't want anything from anyone!"

"It sounds to me like you could use a safe environment to live and work in," I suggested.

I had a feeling about Maggie. She had suffered a lot in life and those who have suffered are often able to help others who face similar trials. "Tell you what," I said to her, "I could use a good apprentice. The pay's not so good, but the benefits are great. You'd be helping a lot of people who could really use a hand up. And you won't have to lie, cheat, steal or manipulate to get what you want. All you'll have to do is just ask, and it will be given to you."

When I still saw some hesitation in her face, I quickly added, "I give you my word: no one will ever make you do what you don't want to do. I believe in everyone having their free will and choice to decide what they want to do."

Maggie's concerns seemed to have eased a little, so I pressed her for an answer. "So, what do you say? Are you with us, Maggie?"

She thought for a minute more and then said, "Well, what about Jo and Suzy? I won't go without them."

Divinely Dysfunctional

I smiled and said, "I wouldn't dream of splitting up the Three Musketeers. Sure, you're all welcome to come. If your goal is to help others, now is as good a time as any to get started."

I was not prepared for Maggie's answer. "Don't worry about the money. I've got a little saved up, and Jo and Suzy have some savings as well. Maybe we can even help fund some of the work you're doing for others."

Wow! What a blessing!

So that's the story of how Maggie and I became such good friends. As time passed, I and my gang of merry men, along with the Three Musketeers, were able to bring joy to the lives of many people. Everywhere we went people came out in record numbers to receive help and counsel, and they were amazed at how this small group was doing such a big work for the cause of humanity.

I rarely got an opportunity to get back home, but then, one day, when we were helping some people not far from my mother's house, I decided that we would all go to her place for dinner. Mom was glad to see me and was also excited to meet the rest of the team. She had heard of the work we were doing and told me she was very proud of her son.

I introduced each of the team to Mom, beginning with Pete, since he was the feisty one of the bunch. Next came the twins, Jimmy and Andy. And then I went on to Jon, Phil, Bart, Matt, Tommy, Jamey, Simon and the two James. Normally I would have introduced the women first, but I knew Mom would love them, so I kept the Three Musketeers until last.

Now I said, "Mom, this is Suzy, the quiet one, Jo, short for Joanna, and Maggie. These ladies, just as the others, have been a tremendous help to me everywhere we've gone." Mom is a hugger, so she had to hug each one, and they all hugged her back.

Following the introductions, we all sat down to eat. Then, after dinner, everyone sort of broke up into groups and began talking. I noticed that Mom and Maggie seemed to be engaged in a lively conversation, so I walked over to where they were in the room and said, "What are you two smiling about?"

"It's girl talk," they both agreed, "so we're sure you wouldn't be interested."

Divinely Dysfunctional

I just smiled and walked away, but from that time on Maggie and Mom were very close. Maggie would go and visit Mom whenever possible, and over the years they grew closer and closer. The result was that Maggie became like a daughter to my mother.

Maggie also developed into a great disciple for the team. No matter how early we had to rise or how late we had to stay up, Maggie was always willing. She would do whatever was necessary, so she fit in perfectly with the group.

Some of the other team members had been quite skeptical of Maggie at first, but they quickly grew to love her as Mom and I did. While Maggie never talked much about what her life had been like back in that little fishing town, everyone new she was glad to be out of there. Her transformation was something to see.

And Maggie's transformation was continuing. When we had first met, she was irritable, edgy and very evasive and untrusting of anyone and everyone. Her long hair had always been tightly braided, and everything about her said that she was unhappy. Now, here she was, laughing and smiling, with her hair down and flowing, and she was willing to give a complete stranger all she had—if it would help them. Maggie had journeyed all the way from a paranoid and perhaps abused schizophrenic hooker into a beautiful woman who found true religion by helping others to overcome their obstacles. She was a great example of how someone can overcome anything if they only believe. There is no doubt about her having been dysfunctional, but now the truth was that she was *Divinely Dysfunctional.*

CHAPTER 10

SOCIALLY DISTORTED

*We hear from others opinions and we
see from others perspectives.*

s Professor Jones approaches the podium, there is a visible sadness in his face. "It is hard to believe," he says, "that we have so quickly come to the end of this series of lectures. I, for one, hate to see them end. They have done so much for each of us. We can never look at the words *dysfunction* or *dysfunctional* in the same light as before. We are all a bit dysfunctional, but, as Dr. Christopher Divine has so aptly shown us, that should not prevent us from being all that we are destined to be.

"Have you appreciated the lectures? If so, please stand up and show Dr. Divine just how much." They all stand and cheer as Dr. Divine takes his place at the podium.

Thank you. As professor Jones has said, this must conclude my series of lectures entitled *"Good Dysfunction,"* and, because of other commitments, I'm afraid I must cut it short here as I conclude.

One meaning of the word *conclude* is "to arrive at a judgement or opinion through reasoning." So then, after reviewing various definitions, being reminded of famous people's lives and hearing stories of my own family's lineage, let's see if we can arrive at an opinion together through reasoning about the term *dysfunctional.*

Again, *dysfunctional* means "to deviate from normal behavior." We have been reminded that no two people ever born were naturally, physically or spiritually exactly alike. Even identical twins are not really identical. So perhaps we can resign ourselves by saying that we are all different from one another, and that is not true dysfunction.

Further, I submit that most of our differences are far beyond our control and, hence, a part of some greater plan. In short, we were each created differently, and that's why we are different from each other. Being different is not a bad thing.

Divinely Dysfunctional

Each of us is a Designer's original, and no one is exempt from this truth. Every single one of our families is made up of flawed, unique and odd individuals. And just maybe your dysfunction or theirs (or both) was by divine design, just like the people whose stories I have told you during these very enjoyable sessions.

I leave you with this thought: Now that we know the truth about being dysfunctional, there can be no more excuses. Get out there and see what the future holds for you. For all you know, yours could quite possibly be the next great success story to be written and talked about. Are you considered to be dysfunctional? If so, the truth is that you are *Divinely Dysfunctional.*"

Remember this: Your dysfunction doesn't determine your destiny, it prepares you for it! God bless you.

Your
dysfunction
doesn't
determine
your
destiny,
it
prepares
you
for
it!

CHAPTER 11

NOW YOU KNOW THE REST OF THE STORY

*A*lthough we have used the stage name Chris Divine, it is important to note, in closing, that our character's family was a depiction from the Holy Bible. Each character was taken from the first chapter of the book of Matthew, and each one represented a family member of the Lord Jesus Christ, or Chris, as He was called here.

Yaakov is the Hebrew name for Jacob, who did, in fact, have twelve sons, including Reuben, Joseph and the youngest, Benjamin. Jacob is said to have actually cheated his brother out of his inheritance and married both of his first cousins, Leah and Rachel.

Jacob's son Judah did impregnate his daughter-in-law Tamar, who was pretending to be a prostitute in order to get him to do so. They did, in fact, have twin boys together.

Ruth and Naomi really did have a tight bond as in-laws who experienced a lot of loss and grief together, but they ultimately shared joy together as well. Ruth married Boaz (whom we call Bo Kingsley) and had a son, and they became ancestors of Jesus.

Please read Matthew 1 to see each character on full display, and then take time to read about their stories of redemption in other parts of the Bible.

The only character not in Jesus's lineage was the last one, Mary Magdalene, here called Maggie. She was His disciple. Unbelievable though it may seem, all of these very imperfect men and women were a planned part of God's earthly family.

It is important also to take notice of the fact that four of the featured women were not Jewish, further illustrating God's design from the beginning to incorporate Gentiles, or non-Jews, into His family. The four non-Jewish women—Tamar (Tammy Martha), Rahab (Rhoby), Ruth (Rue), and Bathsheba (Shelby)—were all central characters in the development of Jesus' earthly bloodline, as indicated in the New Testament's first chapter penned by the apostle Matthew.

The honor given to these four women should, in no way, demean the contributions of other great women of the Bible—women like Eve, Sarah, Miriam, Deborah, Esther and Elizabeth. I believe that by listing these women of somewhat questionable lives and backgrounds the Bible brings hope to every walk of life. It shows us that it doesn't matter as much where you came from as it does where you're heading.

Those of you who know your Bible will, no doubt, have noticed that with some family histories, I chose not to follow the biblical narrative, but, instead, gave the story a more modern slant. This was especially true of the well-known story of Joseph and his coat of many colors. The end result, however, was the same.

Each of these stories is about a real person's life, someone who saw trouble, misfortune, victimization, abuse, abandonment and much more, yet they were not only able to survive, but also to excel in spite of the situations in which they had found themselves. Most of us fail to realize that the highway that leads to a place called Success first began as a rocky dirt path in the middle of place called Nowhere. Every bump, every closed road, all the washed-out bridges, detours and accidents have been accounted for in the journey. All we need to do is keep moving forward and keep believing. Our ultimate destiny is assured.

On many occasions, Jesus would let people know that it was not He who performed a miracle, but rather their faith in the fact that it could still happen. Anytime we see great and extraordinary things happening in the lives of ordinary people (everyday folk, just like you and me), then we can know for a certainty that all things are truly possible.

Too many times we wait and seek the affirmations of others instead of sticking to the task at hand and allowing the accolades to follow the accomplishment. Often what seems to get so many discouraged is the length of time it takes for something to come to fruition. Those who tend to be impatient of the time tend not to understand the process, and everything has a process.

God does everything that He does through a process. Take, for example, when He created Heaven and Earth. He took seven days to create everything, when we all know He could have done it a day or less. But when you consider the process of Creation and all that it must have entailed, a time clock is insignificant to the end result.

Divinely Dysfunctional

The Bible gives the account that God spent the entire first day just making the light the way it should be, ensuring that it wasn't too bright or too dim, that it knew when to turn on and when to turn off, and where it was to begin and end in any given moment. Just maybe this process included a lot more than we know or understand.

On day two of Creation, it was recorded that God made something to separate the space below from the space above (that's what we know as the sky). Since that's all He did that day, making the sky must have been far more detailed than we might imagine.

On day three, it appeared that things were finally going to get rolling off the assembly line. God separated the waters into seas, away from the dry land and planted grass, plants, trees and vegetation of every kind. Then it was over for day three.

So let's review what we've learned thus far from the Creation about process: things are done slowly, one piece at a time. Watch closely and you'll see the latest wrinkle in how one might think things should be done.

There are a lot of people who would have probably created the inhabitants of both the land and sea next. However, God, in His infinite wisdom, saw fit on day four to do it another way and create the sun, moon and stars. "Wow! That is completely different from what I would have done," you might say. And therein lies the problem with the path that our lives are on. We think we know what should be done next, and yet things are being done differently.

There are so many lives that are not aligned with the scheduling of God's process. It wasn't until day six that God created the inhabitants for an environment that He had created three days earlier.

Here's something else we can learn from the creation story: God's process is not like my process. The Bible puts it this way:

> *My thoughts are nothing like your thoughts, ... and my ways are far beyond anything you could imagine.*　　　　Isaiah 55:8, NLT [1]

We have to trust that there was a reason God waited so long before placing someone in an environment that He had already created for them.

Often there exists a natural example that will support

---

1. The Holy Bible, New Living Translation, copyright © 1996, 2004, 2015 by Tyndale House Foundation. Carol Stream, Illinois 60188.

a spiritual truth. Consider the process of getting a fish as a pet. You buy the tank, spread the gravel, place the plants, pour the water, and install the pump, filter and chemicals. Why wouldn't you immediately add the fish? The answer is: because you must allow time for this newly-formed environment to gel together before adding fish, or you will kill them. Yes, God, in His infinite wisdom, knows this, and that's why He waits before giving us that which He has prepared for us.

After all, did not Jesus say: *"I'm on my way to get a room ready for you? ... I'll come back and get you so you can live where I live"* (John 14:3-4, MES [2])? If we can learn to give more thought to allowing the process to be thorough and be less worried about how long it takes, I believe we will find ourselves more satisfied with the end result. Many mistakes are made by trying to rush the process.

Each of our lives represents a work in progress. When you look closely at the life of Jesus, you will see someone who had to overcome numerous obstacles. Which of us had a mother who said she spoke with an angel that told her she was carrying the Creator of the Universe's baby? One could but surmise at the

2. The Message, copyright © 1993, 1994, 1995, 1996, 2000, 2001, 2002 by Eugene H. Peterson

convincing it must have taken for Joseph to marry a woman with such a story. The Bible states that once he got the news that she was pregnant, knowing that the child was not his, he wanted to call the whole thing off (see Matthew 1:19-20). Sure, we know that he did eventually marry her, but I wonder: was he ever truly convinced?

The custom of the times was that men and women worshipped separately. This means that Jesus was with Joseph when He was left behind at the Temple for days on end before ever being missed. Who knows how that relationship was? Talk about ready-made families!

We certainly can't forget the incident of the king wanting Jesus murdered while He was still an infant (see Matthew 2:16). These things and countless others all came before His sixteenth birthday. Clearly we can see from His life that your beginning doesn't have to dictate your ending. That's why the life of Jesus is one of the greatest testaments to the concept that we can all come from a failing home, failing parents, failing opportunities and still end up one of the greatest success stories ever told. The characters in this book are perfect examples of those whose beginning was questionable at best, but when it was all said and done, folks like the prostitute Rahab were given a chance at true happiness with a family and new homeland (see Joshua 2).

Take the would-be porn star, Bathsheba, marrying into the royal family and having a child who would be forever known as one the wisest man to walk the earth: that is what God does (see 2 Samuel 2:12).

Who would have ever guessed that a woman named Tamar, who pretended to be a prostitute in order to sleep with her father-in-law, would ever be considered more righteous than one of the foundational patriarchs of the Jewish religious community (see Genesis 38)?

In all of this, there seems to be a pattern forming which proves the notion that it's not where you start but rather where you end up that counts. So, whenever you feel like things can't possibly turn around for you, just remember:

- Noah was a drunk who saved the world.
- Abraham was an old man whom God called one of His very best friends.
- Jacob began as a con-artist but became a nation of righteous people.

- Joseph was an abused child who became a governor.
- David was an adulterer and murderer who was one of Israel's greatest kings.

Do you need more proof?

- Leah was the ugliest sister yet the most blessed and fruitful.
- Elijah was once suicidal, yet he is known as one of the greatest prophets ever.
- Naomi was a childless widow who became the great-great-great-grandmother of Jesus.
- The Samaritan woman was divorced several times over, and yet she led a whole town to Christ.
- Lazarus was a dead man who became a great disciple.

So, as Chris said in his farewell lecture, no more excuses! Get out there and see what the future holds for you. For all you know, yours could quite possibly be the next great success story to be written and talked about. Are you considered to be dysfunctional? If so, accept the truth, that you are *Divinely Dysfunctional.*

Author's Contact Page

You may communicate directly with the author at the following address:

divinelydysfunctional@gmail.com

www.ingramcontent.com/pod-product-compliance
Lightning Source LLC
LaVergne TN
LVHW011330080426
835513LV00006B/271